Images 28 presents the results of much painstaking deliberation by our panel of well respected (and tough-nosed) industry judges. Their sole task has been to sift through a deluge of entries from the most talented illustrators and to generously identify only the very best from the year.

An *Images* annual is therefore unique.

On the pages that follow you will find out just who are the illustration stars of today – as acknowledged by their peers.

And that's something you won't find anywhere else.

Images 28 published by
The Association of Illustrators
81 Leonard Street London EC2A 4QS
T +44 (0)20 7613 4328
E info@theaoi.com
W www.theAOI.com

Book designed by Atelier Works

Production in China by
Hong Kong Graphics and Printing Ltd
T (852) 2976 0289
F (852) 2976 0292

Acknowledgements
We are grateful for the support of the many organisations
and individuals who contribute to the Images exhibition
and annual:

Our dedicated team of judges for applying their expertise
to the difficult task of selecting this year's work

Nicole Peli for the production of Images 28

Ian Chilvers and Joe Luffman at Atelier Works for their design

Matthew Richardson for the use of his illustrations on the
cover and information pages

Russell Cobb for the use of his illustration on the Images
29 Call for Entries form

Finers Stephens Innocent for their legal advice

Pentagram Design Ltd for their kind support of Images 28
through The Pentagram Award

Stuart Briers for establishing and maintaining the AOI website

All our dedicated casual staff and volunteers for their
invaluable assistance with the competition and exhibition

The Association of Illustrators
AOI Volunteer Council of Management: Francis Blake,
Russell Cobb, Joanne Davies, Leo Duff, Adam Graff, Willi
Gray, Rod Hunt, Alison Lang, Michael Sheehy, Louise Weir

AOI Chair: Michael Bramman

Advisors: Stuart Briers, Edward Eaves, Ruth Gladwin,
Frazer Hudson, Robert Lands, James Marsh, Beth
Pountney, Simon Stern, Fig Taylor

Exhibitions and Events: Rochelle Symons
T +44 (0)20 7739 8901

Images Co-ordinator: Stephanie Alexander
(until February 2004)
T +44 (0)20 7739 8901

Images Co-ordinator/Manager: Silvia Baumgart
(from February 2004)
T +44 (0)20 7613 1467

Membership and Publications: Anna Steinberg,
Derek Brazell & Matt Johnson
T +44 (0)20 7613 4328

Accounts: Paul Hobgen, Ventura Administration Centre
T +44 (0)1622 844 417

The Association of Illustrators, London

COMMISSIONERS SURVEY 2004

Dear Commissioner,

You have now received the new copy of Images 28 – the Best of British Illustration. We believe it is a wonderful book promoting the wealth and new talent of British illustration today. The Association of Illustrators publishes the only jury-selected annual in the UK – a must for any commissioner of illustration.

If you could fill in this questionnaire and return it to the address below it will help us to make a great product even better.

Thank you for supporting the Association of Illustrators.

The AOI Council and staff

IMAGES BOOK

Q.1 **How do you rate the following:**
(1 = poor to 5 = excellent)

	1	2	3	4	5
Design					
Quality of illustrations					
Editorial content					
Practicability					
Format					

Q.2 **What do you think about the content/page layout?**
(please tick more than one box if necessary)

❑ Image-text balance is about right

❑ Too much white space

❑ Images are sometimes too small to recognise details

❑ Image size is balanced and easy to read throughout

❑ Less text information per page would be better

❑ I would like to see the contact details of the illustrator with the image

❑ Index is easy to use

❑ The alphabetical order within the sections is necessary and very useful

❑ The alphabetical order within the sections is not necessary as the index guides you to the image and vice versa

❑ I would like to see more editorial text

❑ I would like to know more about individual illustrators (e.g. short biographies)

❑ I would like to read more detailed descriptions of the brief

❑ I would like to see features on award winners (e.g. profile of illustrator, rough sketches, development of the job, etc)

❑ The information provided is enough and fulfils the purpose of the book

Q.3 **What would you think about the book on CD-Rom to be delivered with the hard copy:**

❑ Exciting

❑ Indifferent

❑ I would very much like to see the multi media work on CD-Rom rather than just individual frames on a printed page

❑ I would use the CD-Rom only

❑ I would still use the hard copy

❑ I would use both depending on the situation

❑ I use the Images file on the AOI website so don't need the CD-Rom

Q.4 **How frequently do you use Images when commissioning illustration?**

- ❑ I use it for 100% of commissions.
- ❑ I use it for 75% of all commissions
- ❑ I use it for more than 50% of commissions
- ❑ I use it for less than 50% of commissions
- ❑ I use it for less than 25% of commissions

Q.4a **What other source do you use when commissioning illustration?**
(please tick more than one box if necessary)

Books:

- ❑ Contact
- ❑ The Artbook
- ❑ Circus
- ❑ Creative Handbook
- ❑ Le Book

Web:

- ❑ AOIimages.com
- ❑ elfande.co.uk (Contact)
- ❑ agency sites
- ❑ individual websites

Other sources:

- ❑ Individual postcards
- ❑ Direct mail
- ❑ Other (please specify)

....

Q.5 **Which is your favourite and most frequently used source book?**

- ❑ Images
- ❑ Contact
- ❑ The Artbook
- ❑ Circus
- ❑ Creative Handbook
- ❑ Le Book

Q.5a **If you think Images is not as good as others we would like to know why.**

Please comment:

....

....

....

Q.6 **Looking at the book, what is your view of the AOI?**
(1 = completely disagree to 5 = completely agree)

	1	2	3	4	5
Professional					
Contemporary					
Efficient					
Represents all illustrators					
Successful in promoting illustration					

GENERAL

Q.7 **When you think about your budget for commissioning photography and illustration what percent goes towards illustration?**

- ❑ Up to 10%
- ❑ 10% to 25%
- ❑ 26% to 50%
- ❑ 51% to 75%
- ❑ 76% to 100%

Q.8 **How often do you commission illustrators?**

- ❑ More than 50 times per year
- ❑ More than 25 times per year
- ❑ 13 to 25 times per year
- ❑ monthly
- ❑ Less than quarterly
- ❑ more

Q.8a **Over the last two years has your illustration budget**

- ❑ increased?
- ❑ decreased?
- ❑ remained stable?

Q.9 **Would you personally like to commission more illustration?**

- ❑ Yes
- ❑ No

Q.10 How do you rate your experience of commissioning illustrators?
(1 = poor to 5 = excellent)

	1	2	3	4	5
reliability					
fulfilled the brief					
value for money					
flexibility					
professionalism					
time keeping					
contribution of own creative ideas					

Q.11 Which of the following prompts you to commission a particular illustrator?

❑ web page

❑ illustrator's mailer

❑ book page

❑ all three

Q.12 With the ease of accessing relevant imagery these days how important is it to you to see a physical portfolio?

❑ Very important

❑ I still like to see portfolios though not essential

❑ I don't see many portfolios

❑ not important

Q.13 Which of the following industry publications do you normally read?

❑ Creative Review

❑ Design Week

❑ Grafik

❑ Eye

❑ AOI Journal

❑ Other (please specify)

....

Q.14 Do you ever use stock illustration in your work?

❑ yes

❑ no

Q.14a If yes, for what reason?

❑ It is easier to find and obtain an image

❑ on instruction from superior

❑ deadline is too short to commission an illustrator

❑ lower cost

❑ other (please specify)

....

Q.15 Do you ever use royalty free illustration in your work?

❑ yes

❑ no

Q.16 Does your company use purchase orders for illustration purchases?

❑ Yes

❑ No

❑ Sometimes

Q.17 Does your company use written contracts for illustration purchases?

❑ Yes

❑ No

❑ Sometimes

ABOUT YOU

Q.18 My job title is

....

Q.19 How old are you?

❑ younger

❑ 21 – 25 years

❑ 26 – 30 years

❑ 31 – 39 years

❑ 40 – 50 years

❑ 51 – 60 years

❑ older

Q.20 Your education

(please tick more than one box if necessary)

❑ Arts foundation course

❑ BA Graphic Design

❑ BA Illustration

❑ MA Graphic Design

❑ MA Illustration

❑ others courses:

....

....

Please write any other comments here:

Thank you for your time!

Please send the questionnaire to
AOI Association of Illustrators
81 Leonard Street
London
EC2A 4QS

You can also complete the questionnaire online.
Visit our website: www.theaoi.com

If you have any questions please don't hesitate to
contact Silvia Baumgart
Tel: 020 7613 1467 or
email: silvia@theaoi.com

contents

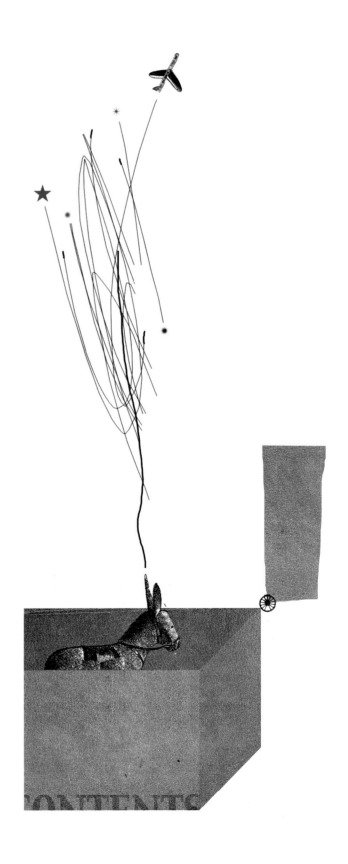

about the **AOI**

The AOI was established in 1973 to advance and protect illustrator's rights and encourage professional standards. The AOI is a non-profit making trade association dedicated to its members' professional interests and the promotion of illustration.

Members consist primarily of freelance illustrators as well as agents, clients, students and lecturers. The AOI is run by an administrative staff responsible to a volunteer Council of Management.

Campaigning

As the only body to represent illustrators and campaign for their rights in the UK, the AOI has successfully increased the standing of illustration as a profession and improved the commercial and ethical conditions of employment for illustrators. The AOI is a member of the Creators Rights Alliance (CRA). It helped to establish the secondary rights arm of the Designers and Artists Copyright Society, (DACS), the UK visual arts collecting society.

Responsible for establishing the right of illustrators to retain ownership of their artwork, the AOI aims to expose and resist rights abuses and exploitative practices within the industry whenever they occur. On behalf of its members, and with their continued support, the AOI can attempt things that it would be difficult or impossible individually. As part of the CRA, for example, the AOI is able to lobby parliament for changes in UK law, aligning it more closely with those of our European neighbours, widely seen as more creator friendly. We are also commissioning further research into the extent of creators rights abuses, with a view to challenging the DCMS, and examining the shortcomings of the new communications bill from a creator's perspective. Currently AOI is working on producing a code of conduct for members' agents to promote good practice within the illustration industry.

Information and support services

Portfolio advice

Members are entitled to a free annual consultation with the AOI's portfolio consultant. Objective advice is given on portfolio presentation, content and suitable illustration markets and agents.

Journal

The AOI Journal is distributed bimonthly to members, keeping them informed about exhibitions, competitions, campaigns and activities in the profession. The Journal is also available to non-members on subscription.

Publications

The AOI publishes Rights: The Illustrator's Guide to Professional Practice, a comprehensive guide to the law for illustrators. It provides detailed advice on how to protect against exploitative practices and contains a model contract for illustrators to use. We also produce Survive: The Illustrator's Guide to a Professional Career which is a comprehensive practical guide to beginning and continuing a career as a professional illustrator. Survive includes information about marketing, ethics, agents and a guide to fees. These publications are available to members at reduced rates.

Client Directories

The AOI currently has three illustration client directories. The Editorial Directory has details of over 200 contacts in the newspaper and magazine industries. The Publishing Directory is a comprehensive list of over 180 important contacts in book publishing. The Advertising Directory has details of over 180 contacts from the world of advertising.

Business advice

Members are entitled to a free consultation with the AOI Chartered Accountant who can advise on accounting, National Insurance, tax, VAT and book-keeping.

Discounts

Members receive discounts on AOI events, publications and a number of art material suppliers nationwide.

Legal advice

Full and Associate members receive advice on ethics and contractual problems, copyright and moral right disputes.

Return of artwork stickers

Available to AOI members only. These stickers help safeguard the return of artwork.

Students and new illustrators

Our seminars and events combined with the many services we offer, can provide practical support to illustrators in the early stages of their career.

Events

The AOI runs an annual programme of events which include one day seminars, evening lectures and thematic exhibitions. These include talks by leading illustrators as well as representatives from all areas of the illustration field, and cover such subjects as children's book illustration, aspects of professional practice, new technologies and illustrators' agents. AOI members are entitled to discounted tickets.

Membership

To request further information or a membership application form please telephone +44 (0)20 7613 4328

Website

Visit our website at www.theAOI.com for details of the Association's activities, including samples from current and past Journals, details of forthcoming events, the AOI's history and on-line portfolios.

Patrons

Glen Baxter
Peter Blake
Quentin Blake
Raymond Briggs
Chloe Cheese
Carolyn Gowdy
Brian Grimwood
John Hegarty
David Hughes
Shirley Hughes
Sue Huntley
Mick Inkpen
Donna Muir
Ian Pollock
Gary Powell
Tony Ross
Ronald Searle
Paul Slater
Ralph Steadman
Simon Stern
Peter Till
Janet Woolley

foreword

Michael Bramman

With the AOI celebrating thirty years of campaigning for illustrators' rights it seems an appropriate time to assess its achievements and even to indulge in a little crystal ball gazing. While its fortunes have mirrored the economic situations of the times it has steadfastly advanced its objectives. From its formation by a small group of artists and agents it has vigorously defended illustrators' rights to maintain copyright of their work. Previously to 1975 commissioners took it for granted that they owned the artwork. When it came to light that the law sided with the artists, the AOI's publicising of this eventually resulted in the curtailment of this practice.

Now once again some companies are attempting to reinstate ownership and total rights with little or no added compensation. The digital capacity to store and transmit large amounts of images has presented a new opportunity to recycle work. While the offer from a stock house of a large fee for the ownership of a portfolio may seem to be tempting, the ultimate result will be a diminishing of commissions and new creative work. I'm sure I'm preaching to the converted in these pages but this Faustian pact is something to be resisted.

Since the last exhibition there has been a continued surge of interest in the AOI. The Top Ten illustrators as voted by the AOI published in The Independent on Sunday, Creative Week ran an article on our 30th and there have been requests for interviews from numerous sources. Hopefully this signals an increased interest in illustration and encourages our ambition to see a major national exhibition of 30 years of illustration.

We continue to work with the Creators Rights Alliance and sent a delegate to Association Professional of Illustrators in Valencia for a two day conference, First Illustrator's Transnational Rendezvous. We maintain contact with the Society of Illustrators, Graphic Artists Guild and the Illustrators Partnership in the US.

The AOI has held several sell out events, the last at the time of writing being the

Illustration in the Digital Age held at the RCA. Many of our members participated in the Arts Council's Big Art Week by visiting local schools to talk to the pupils about working as an illustrator and setting up and monitoring an art project. Members also donated work to the charity Paintings in Hospitals. Following the exhibition at the Sheridan Russell Gallery the work went to brighten children's wards across the country. We also again supported the Big Draw and continue to promote drawing programmes in colleges. The V&A Illustration Awards gave a touch of style to the close of 2003.

Images 28 with Matthew Richardson's cover chosen from among the highest point scores reflects the diversity and power of illustration as selected by independent judges and coupled with the AOI web site makes a formidable promotional tool and an unrivalled record of British illustration produced since the last exhibition. I would like to thank all those who worked for its success.

And finally a message from one of the truly great British illustrators.

"… before a guardian angel, the AOI, who with flaming sword tries to cut through inertia, exploitation, pinchers of copyright (and originals) and try to knead the mess into an homogeneous whole. Here's to the next thirty years." Ronald Searle

A creative and productive future to you all.

Michael Bramman
AOI Chair

introduction

Lawrence Zeegen

Let's think about the environment. When I say environment I really mean our environment as illustrators; the space that we occupy both physically and mentally. Resist the temptation to skip straight to the images, and give this some thought…

Where is it that you create your work? Try to think geographically and physically as well as mentally. All three spaces, I believe, help to determine and influence the way in which we work and the kind of work that we create.

Let's start with geography. I've heard the arguments before, even contributed to them myself in the past; geographic location no longer matters. We have mobile phones, email, the web and broadband so illustrators can now work anywhere. True, we are able to deliver projects to clients from almost any spot on the globe, we no longer have to be a stone's throw away or within a courier's pick-up zone - but is that really the complete picture? Sure, we can have art supplies on 'next day delivery', we can download software updates in an instant, we can 'Google Image Search' (425,000,000 at last count) for reference and promote our services with web-based portfolios. But does that really mean that geography and location count for nothing? I think not.

We all need more than digital inspiration, the easy one-click access to referencing an image or even an idea or solution. I get a buzz from seeing, hearing, breathing in and being part of my environment, not just where I live and work but places that I travel to and visit. They all feed into my creative image making. I get ideas whilst walking through urban spaces, find reference materials at street markets, see a particular combination of colours in shop signage or just get a kick from coming across some stencilled graffiti. For me the city is the inspiration that can't be delivered via my laptop. I need real life.

This may all sound a little obvious, but I get the sense that the digital promise has failed to live up to every expectation.

I recently started, and completed, an editorial illustration commission on a flight from Heathrow to JFK; I had almost turned the job down but my yearning to discover if I could be a 21st century mobile creative got the better of me. The notion of calling up creativity to order, resolving a job to a very tight deadline and attempting to step into the unknown, strangely appealed to me, as did the fee paying for the flight. The illustration was ok, I have to admit it was not the best job I've ever done, and although my trusty Powerbook and extra battery did not let me down, something was not right. The geography was all wrong; I was in mid-air, I had no visual source of inspiration apart from a bundle of images saved on my hard drive, I had no reference to draw from conceptually and nothing to draw from visually. These drawbacks showed in the illustration.

So, moving on from geographic environment, let's consider the physical space. This is the space that you actually work in; draw, paint, print, collage, both in traditional and digital mediums and any combination of each of these. Illustration for many can be a solo experience: the kitchen table, the spare bedroom or a studio in the attic. Home-working was a phrase that could have been invented for the illustrator but is it the most conducive location for the creation of work or is it that financial considerations have forced this practice? Art school was never like this; studio discussion, critiques and seminars played a huge part in creative image making. Back to my flight, on route to New York; I can say that it was easily the least creative environment I had ever worked in, I was trapped in a pretty small space, belted in, the tiny pull-out table and lighting less than ideal.

But more than that, I had no opportunity to discuss the piece mid-illustration with the art director or with studio colleagues. My fellow passengers were plugged into the movie and I was on my own.

Encouragingly, despite economics, it appears that many illustrators have returned to the shared studio set-up; recognising the need for input into the creative process from their peers, through sharing ideas and thoughts as well as facilities and even client base. A new generation recognise the rewards of working alongside each other, often basing their set-up on re-creating that good old art school experience or, increasingly and depressingly, the experience that they wished their time in education to have been.

What it is not clear right now is exactly where the art school experience is heading. Sadly, too many art and design courses have abandoned access to the studio as a full-time right. Ever-increasing student numbers and never-increasing accommodation has ensured that this can be a no-win situation. Hot-desking has not worked for a number of 'stack-them-high-sell-them-cheap' courses. Introducing students to the concept of home-working has been the fail-proof method for managing the 'numbers' game. Meanwhile, at some of these institutions, much of the communication between students and peers and students and staff has had to rely on the digital; email tutorials and on-line discussion instead of real head-to-head dialogue. The allure of the digital has started to fade; it was never meant to replace real communication, surely.

It is the theme of communication that brings us to the third environment; the space that describes mentally or conceptually where you work and the approach that you adopt. This is tougher to determine. Illustration has always existed in a pretty interesting place, occupying an area that sits between art and design. Illustration has never truly been considered an adjunct of art with a capital 'A', nor wholly existed without the prop that is graphic design.

Artists drive their own work, their own projects; they instigate the investigation, they formulate the subject matter, they choose the medium, the outlet and manage the process. This freedom supports self-expression, the creation of a personal visual language and if wholly successful leads to the unexpected, pushing the discipline into new areas, breaking boundaries and enlightening both artist and audience. Designers, meanwhile, have an altogether different starting point, they solve given problems, responding to a client's needs; they create visual solutions; they analyse, organise and present information. Design has a particular purpose and fulfils a functional role. Where does illustration fit into either of these descriptions?

With art and design existing so far apart conceptually, I believe, it is the area at the very edges of both disciplines where new forms of illustration can thrive and evolve. The best new work needs and feeds from both art and design and through these relationships can offer an alternative to the

mainstream. It is the understanding of how to utilise a range of approaches to creativity, witnessed across both art and design; that can empower the illustrator. Leading and initiating projects, taking risks, breaking with convention, even seizing control should not sound like revolutionary tactics but more like a game plan for moving the subject forward.

New Illustration does not sit and wait for the designer's telephone call to kick-start a commission; it is out there creating projects, shows and exhibitions, publications, web sites, prints and posters; it is being proactive. The best of new illustration generates and collaborates. *New Illustration* works *with* designers and clients and not *for* them; there is now an equality that has taken a number of years to claw back. Let's not forget how smug design had been because it had embraced and claimed the digital as its own from the start. True, Old Illustration had tried to pretend that the digital never even existed but that was yesteryear; with the digital mastered there is now a new respect for the craft and skills of *New Illustrators*.

Illustration is still going through its dramatic re-birth, this is a crucial time for the discipline and for the AOI itself, thirty years old this year. New approaches, new scenarios, new challenges, new problems will confront New Illustration and potentially difficult times still lay ahead. New Illustration must capitalise on the opportunities being created, being carved out and the AOI can help spear-head that attack. The bigger landscape that New Illustration exists within may be out of our control but the environment that we work within remains within our domain. And when I say environment, I mean all three environments.

Lawrence Zeegen
Academic Programme Leader
Communication and Media Arts
University of Brighton

judges of images

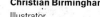

Advertising

Katie Grogan
Art Buyer
Abbot Mead
Vickers BBDO

John Hegarty
Chairman & Worldwide
Creative Director
Bartle Bogle Hegarty

Dave Kelsall
Art Editor
Internet Magazine

Andy Smith
Illustrator

Ralph Steadman
Illustrator

Books

Simon Bishop
Art Editor
BBC Wildlife Magazine

Jason Ford
Illustrator

Craig Mitchell
Art Director
Women & Home

Christopher Sharrock
Dean at
Camberwell College
Illustrator/writer

Michael Sheehy
Illustrator

Donna Thynne
Senior Art Editor
OUP

Children's books

Christian Birmingham
Illustrator

Mark Hayman,
Assistant Art Director
Daily Express

Will Hill
Senior Lecturer
Illustration &
Graphic Design
APU

Bee Willey
Illustrator

Kate Wilson
Managing Director
MacMillan
Children's Books

Year 6 Students
Soho Parish School

judges of images

Design

New media

Editorial

Student

Unpublished

Pete Avery
Freelance Art Director

Sarah Brass
Head of Buying
& Merchandising
Whittard's of Chelsea

Babette Cole
Illustrator

Martin Harrison
Design Editor
Travel & Money
The Times

David Hitch
Illustrator

Jane McCarten
Editor
Connect-The Union
for Professionals
in Communications

Sara Ramsbottom
Art Editor
BBC Parenting Magazine

Jonathan Anstee
Art Editor
Computer Active

Damian Gascoigne
Animation Director
Picasso Pictures

Tom Morgan-Jones
Illustrator

Ian Murray
Illustrator

Mark Wagstaff
Art Editor
Mojo

Andy Baker
Illustrator

Philip Carter
Creative Director
Carter Wong Tomlin

Una Corrigan
Deputy Head
of Graphics
The Economist

David Driver
Head of Design
& Assistant Editor
The Times

Chris Riddell
Illustrator/author

Debra Zuckerman
Creative Director
Zuckerman

Stephanie Fenner
Art Editor
Community Care

Richard Llewellyn
Art Editor
Computer Arts

Hannah MacDonald
Editorial Director
Ebury Press

Katherina Manolessou
Illustrator

Axel Scheffler
Illustrator

Graham Carter
Illustrator

Ian Hughes
Mousemat Design

Mark Parry
Art Director
Personnel
Publication Ltd

Tony Ross
Illustrator

Chris Sanderson
Creative Director
Viewpoint

Dane Wilson
Head of Design
TES

About the **illustrations**

M   Medium
B   Brief
C   Commissioned by
F   Firm

Awards

 Gold

 Silver

 Bronze

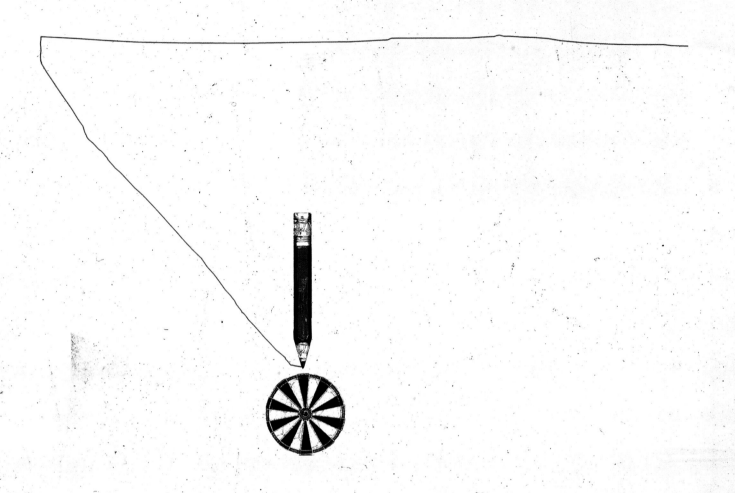

Advertising
Gold award winner

Henry Obasi
Human Conversion

M Digital

B To create a series
   of 12 illustrations
   showing the
   transformation of
   Playstation 2 games
   player via their
   interaction with
   the console

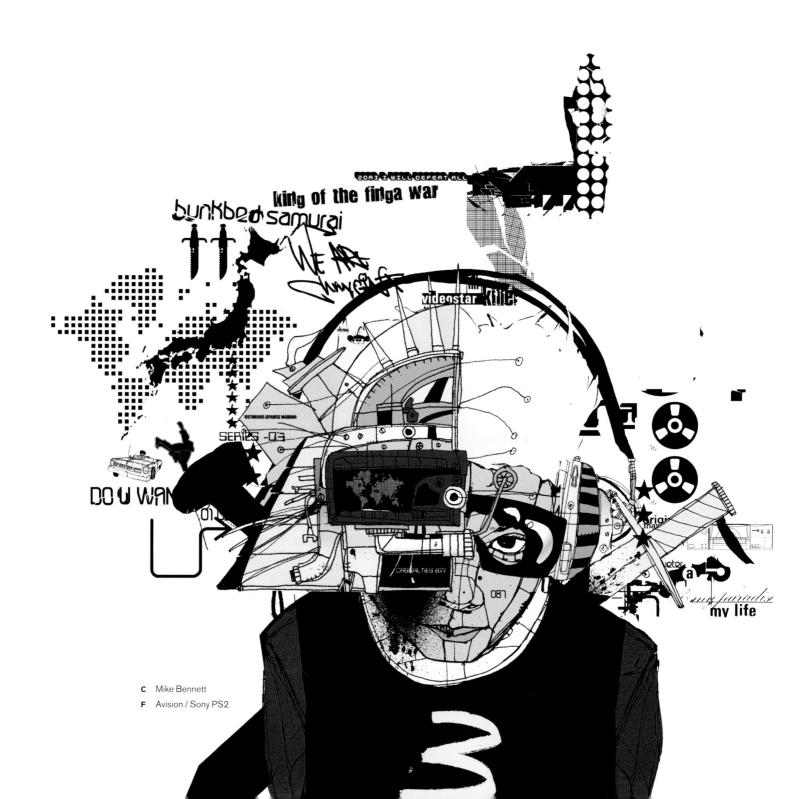

C Mike Bennett

F Avision / Sony PS2

Jonas Bergstrand
Untitled 1
M   Digital
B   Caricatures of
Ozzy Osborne,
Chris Morris,
Keifer Sutherland
and Sarah Jessica
Parker. All watching
TV together

C   Daniel Coupe
F   Radio Times

Jonas Bergstrand
Untitled 2

M Digital

B One of several
images promoting
Eurostar in general
as well as pushing
specific offers

C Lisa-Marie Dickinson

F TBWA London

Untitled 3

M Digital

B One of a series
of images showing
continental
environments with a
hint of railway tracks -
style: Art Deco

Jonathan Burton

Mini / BMW

M Mixed media

B To illustrate the
national campaign
'Look at my Mini'
for Billboards

C Lisa-Marie Dickinson

F TBWA London

C Jane Briers

F WCRS

Graham Carter
BUPA

M Mixed media

B To create a series
of 10 images to
heighten awareness
of BUPA's current
health services

F W.C.R.S

Russell Cobb
Saab 1

M Acrylic

B To produce a series
of fun, quirky and
inventive icons
to promote Saab
car dealerships,
responding to key
words such as
speed, grip, build
and suspension

Barry Downard
Mikado

M Photo-montage

B Achieve powerful
images to evoke
the power of opera,
combining the surreal
with the classic

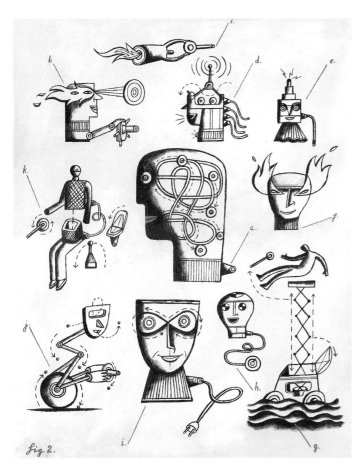

C Ben Vickers

F BMB Ltd

C Rodd Whitney

F Cause Design

Max Ellis

Howard's
Countryside Jaunt

M Digital

B Develop a caricature
of Howard and
create a world for him

Howard the Magician

M Digital

B Further develop
Howard for the Halifax

C Tony Dell

F DLKW

Darren Hopes
Road to
Enlightenment
M Mixed media
B Mini driver seeks road
to enlightenment.
Realises it is not
the A263. The End

Matt Lee
Surprise! Surprise!
M Mixed media
B A mailout for Orange
to promote the use
of text messaging
as a surprise gift

C Angelo/Jon Cole
F EHS Brann

C Paul Lipman
F Craik Jones

Ray Smith
How to Fake it
as a Photographer

M Digital

B To demonstrate
light-heartedly,
ways of faking it
as a photographer
outlined in the booklet
accompanying the
Channel 4 series
'Faking It'

Bob Venables
The All-Natural
Bottle Blonde

M Acrylic

B To create 1920's
style German beer
poster to reflect
the authenticity
and tradition of the
Lowenbrau beer

C James Turnham
F 4 Creative

C Jeff Suthons
F Refresh UK /
Lowenbrau

Louise Weir
We Can't Do
This...but...

M Acrylic

B Abbey National
summer campaign
strapline: we can't
give you...but we
can...showing
idealised solutions
to common summer
'problems' ie. getting
space on a very
crowded beach

C Abbey National
F KLP Euro RSCG

Christopher Wormell
Pebbles

M   Linocut

B   Part of a series of
    posters to promote
    Adnams as 'Beer
    from the Coast'

C   Dave Dye

F   Campbell Doyle Dye

Design and new media
Gold award winner

Ian Whadcock
Traffic Jam
M   Digital
B   To illustrate the
benefits of home
working via
Broadband etc.
The same figure
shown driving in a
traffic jam on cover
and then in the same
position working from
home on the inside

C   Jonathan Sant
F   Worth Group

A. Richard Allen
Up the Creek

M Ink & digital

B Produce an image
for a show themed
around Greenpeace's
'Save or Delete'
campaign highlighting
political indifference
to the plight of
the rainforest

Andrew Baker
Smart Building

M Digital

B To produce
graphics for a
pop-up building,
showing how
it can be made
intelligent through
the installation of
new technology

C Sarbjit Girn /
Brenda Ramsey

F Greenpeace

C Marcella Di Mare

F Nanook

Beach
Ghetto Fabulous
Refrigeration
M Flash animation
B Bring gangsta rap
fridge magnets to
life in a funky and
entertaining way

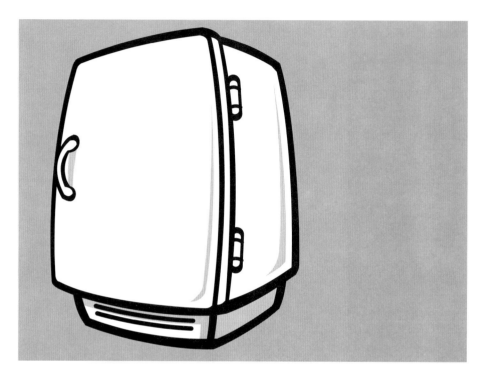

C Huw Casson
F Gangsta Magnets

Paul Bommer
The Shoreditch
Map-April (detail)

M Digital

B To convey some
of the history and
landmarks of the
Shoreditch area
and in particular
indicate the arrival
of Spring

C Robert Smith

F The Shoreditch
Map Company

Fred Brilliant
Santa Wrap
M   Mixed media
B   A seasonal image
    suitable for tiling
    into a downloadable
    desktop pattern

C   Tim Spear
F   Now Wash
    Your Hands

Mick Brownfield
Brand Analysis
M Gouache
B Depict the notion
that brand has
personality that
can be analysed

C David Freeman
F WPP
Atticus Journal

Greg Clarke
Nutcracker
M   Mixed media
B   Illustration for
    a Christmas card

C   Tazmin Coleman
F   Art in Design

Russell Cobb
Working From Home

M Acrylic

B One of a series of
cards promoting
creative director,
copywriter and writer
Simon Carbery. No.1
illustrating the perils
of being at home

C Simon Carbery

F Simon Carbery Ltd.

Jonathan Cusick
Cadbury / Coronation
Street - Flake

M Acrylic

B Character designs
for animated TV
sponsorship ident,
in which a mumsy-
type replaces the
classic 'flake' beauty,
whilst her son
struggles through
the flake music

C Nicola Evans

F EURO RSCG
WNEK Gosper

Jonathan Cusick
Cadbury / Coronation
Street - Heroes
M Acrylic
B Character and
endframe designs
for animated TV
sponsorship ident
in which a 'major',
skinny man and Sikh
play pranks on each
other whilst playing
dominoes

C Nicola Evans
F EURO RSCG
WNEK Gosper

Cadbury / Coronation
Street - Roses

M Acrylic

B Character and
endframe designs
for animated TV
sponsorship ident
in which a grandad
encourages his
pet budgie to talk

C Nicola Evans

F EURO RSCG
WNEK Gosper

Barry Downard
Creative People
M Photo-montage
B Represent 'creative
people' category for
an industry related
recruitment agency

C Bernadette Sturley
F The Recruitment
Business

Sara Fanelli

M Collage

B Effect of paper
manufacturing on
the environment

C Anna Karin Sundin

F Bark Design

David Fathers
The Visitors Map

M Digital

B To totally redraw
   the visitors map,
   electronically, in
   layers, thus enabling
   rapid amendments
   as new features
   are added

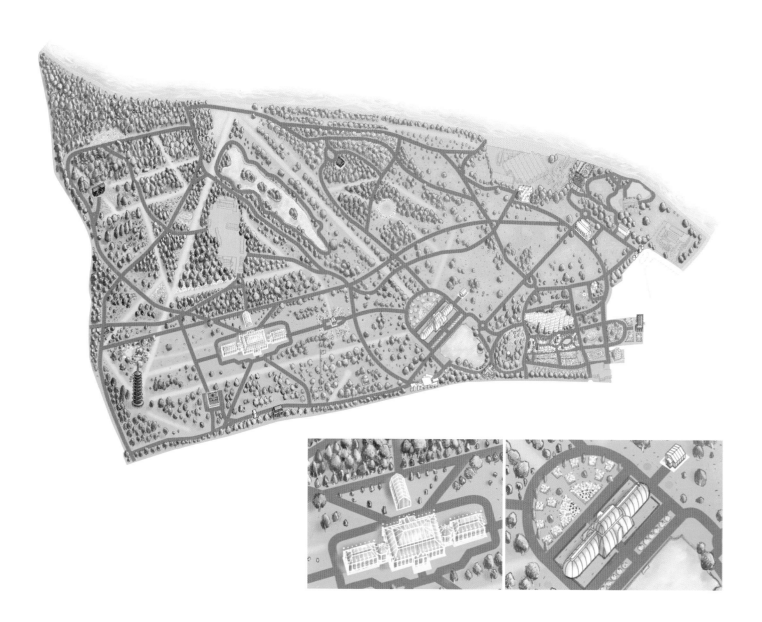

C Media Resources
F Royal Botanic
   Gardens Kew

**Design and
new media**
Silver award winner

Sarah Gibb
Harrods Characters
M Watercolour & ink
B To create a series
of characters to
promote Harrods

C Mark Briggs
F Harrods

Nick Hardcastle
Oliver Cromwell
Departing from
Norwich

M Pen and ink
plus watercolour

B One of a series of
cards depicting the
Norfolk railway scene
in the days of steam

C Kim Hutchins
F Letter Box
Designs Ltd

Jo Hassall
Larousse

M Mixed media

B To provide artwork
which broadly
illustrates the French
publisher's main
outputs ie. youth
encyclopedias,
foreign languages
and practical life

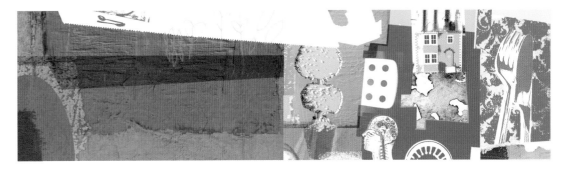

C Sylvie Goy

F Z & Co

42

Peter Horridge
Le Saint Geran
Mermaid

M Pen and ink
(line and wash)

B Produce a calligraphic
illustration of a
mermaid, one of a
set used for Le Saint
Geran Hotel Mauritius
identity print items

**Design and
new media**
Bronze award winner

Le Saint Geran Marlin

M Pen and ink
(line and wash)

B Produce a calligraphic
illustration of a marlin,
one of a set used for
Le Saint Geran Hotel
Mauritius identity
print items

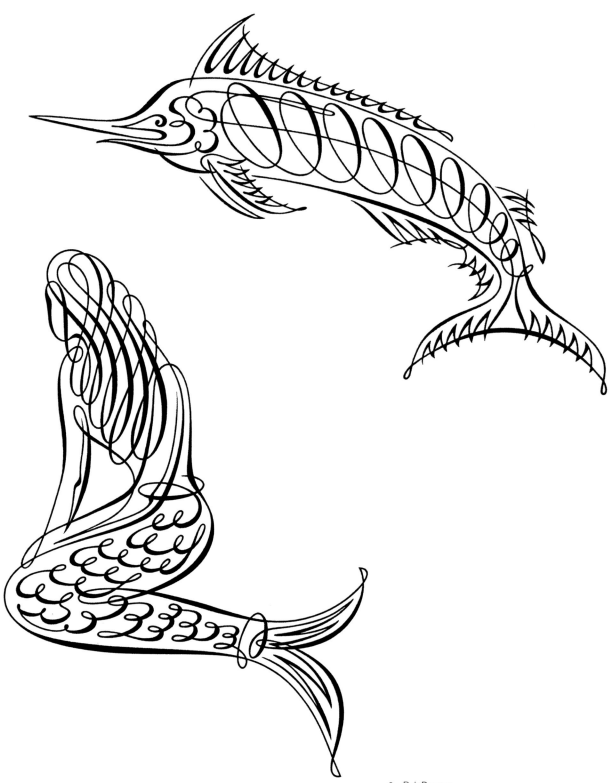

C Rob Duncan
F Pentagram

Le Saint Geran
Triton Shell
M Pen and ink
(line and wash)
B Produce a calligraphic
shell, one of a set
of illustrations for
Le Saint Geran Hotel
Mauritius identity
print items

Le Saint Geran
Hibiscus
M Pen and ink
(line and wash)
B Produce a calligraphic
illustration of Hibiscus,
one of a set used for
Le Saint Geran Hotel
Mauritius identity
print items

Mark Hudson
Skyescape
M   Biro / digital
B   Create a magical
    British snowscape
    for use on Christmas
    cards abroad

C   Clare Jenne
F   Calamansi

Ian Murray

Mr Dog Loves You

M Mixed media / digital

B Produce a set of
images which will
appeal to a young
Japanese audience.
They will be sent
to friends and family
via mobile phones

Robbie Rover

M Mixed media / digital

B Produce a set of
images which will
appeal to a young
Japanese audience.
They will be sent to
friends and family
via mobile phones

Hello Bird

M Mixed media / digital

B Produce a set of
images which will
appeal to a young
Japanese audience.
They will be sent to
friends and family
via mobile phones

C Ben Tanaka

F Taito Corp. Japan

Garry Parsons
Rubadub Pet Foods
M Acrylic
B Healthy, happy,
   hungry pets for
   a series of new
   pet food packets

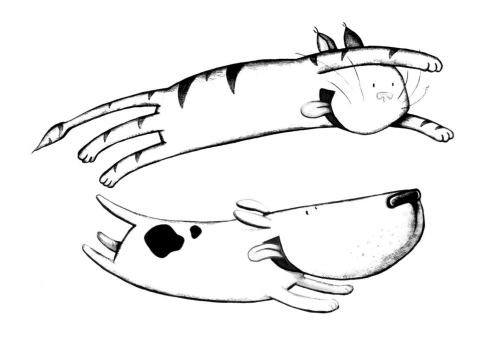

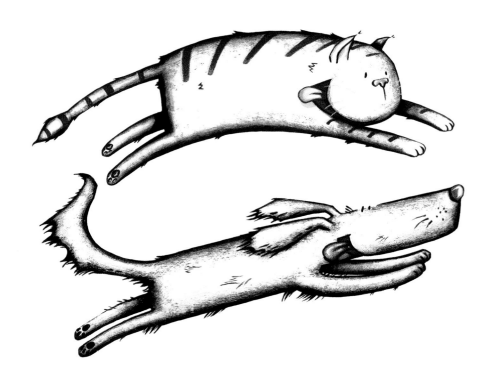

C Affinity
F Wolf Olins

Simon Pemberton
New Voice

M Mixed media

B To produce a bold
and arresting image
for in-store signage
at Blackwell's books
for the aspiring
new writers section
new voices

F Enterprise IG

Ian Pollock
The Devil of
Over-Regulation
M Ink
B The devil of
over-regulation
to safeguard the
pensions industry

C Vicky Oliver
F Philosophy for
DAC Magazine

Ashley Potter
Newlyweds

M Mixed media

B Title series for
a reality TV show,
'Newlyweds',
following two
celebrities as they
get married and
come to terms with
'real' married life

Paul Powis
Le Fleuve II

M Oils

B To produce a tranquil
soft focused image
of a river in twilight

C Mario Cavalli

F Colonymedia .co.uk

C Glyn Washington

F Washington Green

Harriet Russell
Don't confuse
your hairbrush
with a hedgehog

M Collage and digital
B Image for Central
Illustration Agency
calendar on the
theme 'hair do's
and hair don'ts'

Don't confuse your hairbrush with a hedgehog

C Louisa St. Pierre
F Central Illustration
Agency

Colin Shearing
Peter Pan Stamps

M Pencil sketches
digitally coloured

B To create a magical
and engaging
sequence of images
inspired by the
characters from
J.M.Barrie's story
of Peter Pan

C Jane Ryan
F Royal Mail

Michael Sheehy
Budget Cuts

M Mixed media

B Funding for research
and development
is often cut before
the end of the
financial year

Czeslaw Slania
Pillar to Post

M Intaglio

B To engrave images
of pillar boxes
through their 150
year history in order
to utilise the intaglio
print process

C Mary Beth Cadwell

F Storage

C Jane Ryan

F Royal Mail

Paul Slater
Codebreakers

M   Acrylic

B   Depict that beer
advertising has
always had a set
of visual codes that
can be deciphered

Nobby Sprouts
Failing Eyesight

M   Mixed media

B   Follow agency script
about life's medical
shortfalls

C   David Freeman

F   WPP
Atticus Journal

C   Mario Cavalli

F   colonymedia.co.uk

Darrell Warner
Iris
M Watercolour &
coloured pencil
B To produce a series
of traditional botanical
illustrations with a
contemporary feel,
incorporating a heart
within the subject

C Lizzie Spivey
F Heart of the Garden

Peter Warner
Border Collie

M   Watercolour

B   VetVits Flexi-Joints
Packaging. Design for
a small supplement
pack, to highlight the
dog's flexibility, vitality
and energy against
a soft non-specific
background, masked
by various circular
design elements

C   Mark Whyte

F   Healthspan

Paul Wearing
Diners
M Digital
B Large scale print
commissioned to
hang in restaurant
areas of Target. From
a series of artworks
based on the theme of
cafe life and shopping

C Wayne Talley
F Fame Retail

Energy 2   Energy 3

M Digital

B Two in a series of 3
artworks to illustrate
all aspects of Elexon's
technology, from
information exchange
to all forms of energy
production and supply

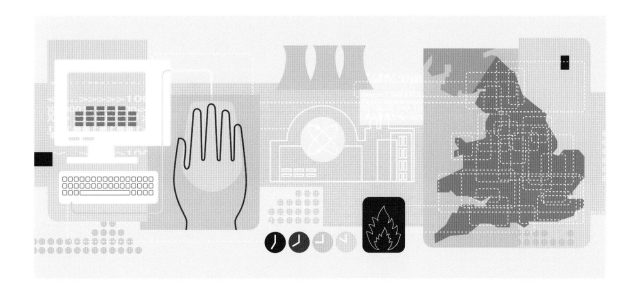

C Jonathan Cook

F The Work Room

Louise Weir

Flesh and Bone

M Acrylic

B Illustrating the journey
of Mankato through
a unique environment
which is neither real or
unreal. Flesh relates
to his mortal state
at the start of his
dreamlike journey.
Bone is a reference
to his dog

Safe as Houses

M Acrylic

B To reflect the isolation
of Mankato in a bleak
unsettling setting.
The feeling of 'open
space' mirrors the
big production of the
single. A homage to
the previous painting
appears in each to
reinforce the concept
of a journey

C Chris Harrison

F Balance Design

Wasted

M Acrylic

B To illustrate the
dreamlike mood of
reflection and calm
the morning after
taking drugs, being
so sensitive to your
environment it almost
becomes you and
vice versa

Bee Willey
Any Time, Any
Place, Any Book

M Mixed media

B To convey the title
sentence for a middle
range children's
books audience (9-13)

C Edgardo Zaghini

F Book Trust

Editorial
Gold award winner

Olivier Kugler
Portrait of
Jonathan Franzen

M Pencil & digital
manipulation

B To produce a portrait
of Jonathan Franzen
for the cover of The
Guardian's REVIEW
supplement

C Roger Browning

F The Guardian

A. Richard Allen

Greatness

M Ink & digital

B Article about how the unlikeliest of people with a little encouragement can become 'Great Men'

How to Drink Cocktails

M Ink & digital

B Humorous article describing the perils of drinking cocktails

Pet Presents

M Ink & digital

B Finding appropriate Christmas presents for pets

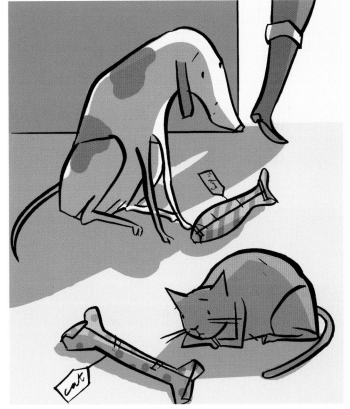

C Sam Freeman

F The Big Issue

C Maggie Murphy

F The Guardian

C Maggie Murphy

F The Guardian

Kenneth Andersson
Lionguy
M Digital
B About a guy who
   thinks he's a Lion

C Paul Tainsley
F Sunday Times
   Magazine

Kenneth Andersson
Silverdrop
M   Digital
B   For The Guardian
    weekly magazine
    for an article about a
    new health 'medicine'
    silverdrops

Andrew Baker
Taking Cell Samples
M   Digital
B   To illustrate the
    art of taking cell
    samples from skin

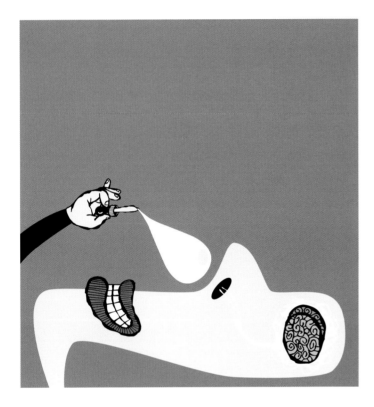

C   Maggie Murphy
F   The Guardian

C   Alison Lawn
F   Reed Business
    Information Ltd

66

Andrew Baker

How to Make
an Organ

M Digital

B To illustrate the art
of moulding unformed
cellular material
into organs for
use in transplants

Monkey Arm
& Robot Arm

M Digital

B To illustrate an
experiment in which
scientists linked a
monkey's brain to
technology which
allows a robot arm to
replicate the
monkey's own arm
movements

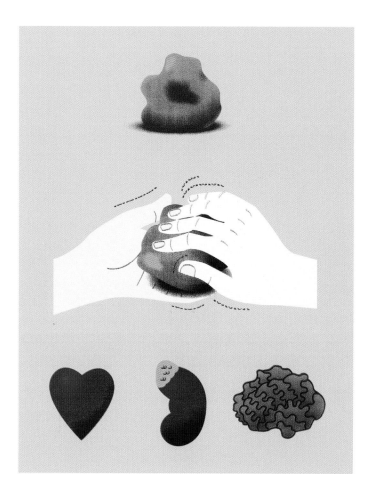

C Alison Lawn

F Reed Business
Information Ltd

Simon Bartram
Lip Service

M Acrylic

B To illustrate an
article about a
woman employed
by the police to up
read surveillance
footage of criminals

Paul Blow
Less Talk -
More Action

M Mixed media

B In business, rather
than sitting around
discussing strategy,
it is better to get out
there and take action

C Martin Colyer

F Reader's Digest

C Eric Siry

F Business 2.0
Magazine

Paul Blow
Crossed Legs

M Mixed media

B In the US pregnant
women are fearful
of giving birth at
weekends due to
inaccurate studies
during the 1970's

Paul Bommer
How To Embarrass
Yourself

M Digital

B To illustrate a piece
by Guy Browning
on how to really show
yourself up in public

C David Armario

F David Armario Design

C Maggie Murphy

F The Guardian

Paul Bommer
Mind the Gaffe

M Digital

B To illustrate an article
by psychologist
Adrian Furnham
on the motives and
meanings behind
giving and receiving
Christmas presents

C Graham Tuckwell

F Financial Times

Paul Bommer

Directory Enquiries	Self Inventory
M Digital	M Digital
B To illustrate a piece on the confusion over choice and charging regarding the new directory enquiries options replacing BT's 192 service	B To illustrate an article on computer software to help record your home contents for insurance purposes

C Suzanne Taylor	C Neil Darby
F Which? Magazine	F Which? Magazine

Stuart Briers
Contraceptive Patch
M Digital
B To accompany an
article about the new
contraceptive patch
available for women

C Natalie Huke
F Express Newspapers

Nigel Buchanan

Pottery Class

M Gouache

B It's Jonny Vegas - but
not as we know him!
This comedy series
saw him condemned
to a hellish existence
as a night-school
pottery teacher

Jubilee Celebration

M Gouache

B Three occupants
of three flats come
together in this
drama to celebrate
the jubilee. A portrait
of very different
individuals linked
by a single event

C Sara Ramsbottom

F Radio Times

Editorial
Silver award winner

Jonathan Burton
White Stripes
M Mixed media
B Illustrate review of
the White Stripes
album 'Elephant'
as a pastiche of
'American Gothic'

C Mark Wagstaff
F Mojo Magazine

Bill Butcher

Disaster

M Digital

B To convey the fact
that despite events
of September 11th,
many companies have
holes in their continuity
arrangements

From Fear
to Modernity

M Digital

B 3 books reviewed on
the subject of terror
and the war on terror.
The illustration was
trying to give a view
of them

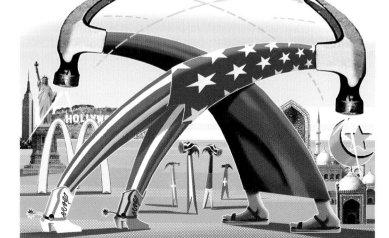

C John Bradley

F Financial Times

C Andy Chappin

F Financial Times

Marina Caruso
Top 50 Corporate
Video Makers

M Digital

B Front cover and inside
article of televisual
magazine to illustrate
top 50 corporate
video and film makers.
Annual feature

C Charlotte Jagger

F Centaur
Communications

Miles Cole
Technology -
Good Vs Bad
M   Digital
B   Illustrate how
technology can
be a force for
good and evil

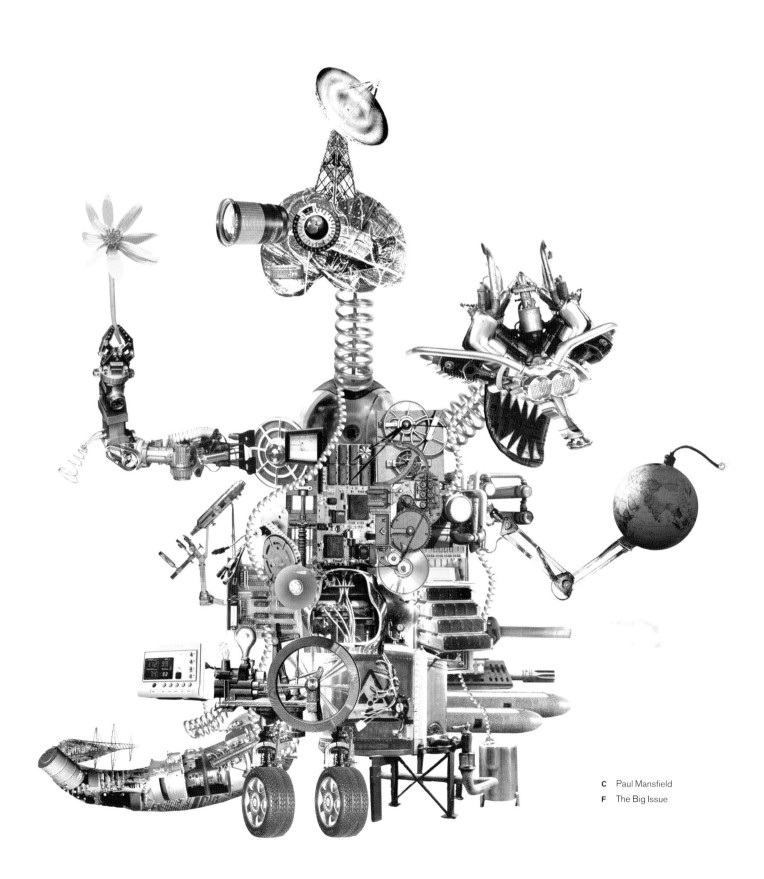

C   Paul Mansfield
F   The Big Issue

Matthew Cook

Soldier by a Wall

M Watercolour

B To record the
conflict in Iraq
as the official
Times war artist

Soldier in a Gas Mask

M Pen and ink

C David Driver

F The Times
Newspaper

Paul Cox
The Angel Tree
M Watercolour & ink
B A narrative piece
about a garden
designer's search
for a rich client, to
find the oldest olive
tree in the world

C Martin Colyer
F Reader's Digest

Brian Cronin

All their own work? Big Fat Problem

M Ink on paper **M** Ink on paper

B The use of websites **B** Childhood obesity
that answer all of a is on the increase
student's questions
is on the increase -
Is it cheating?

C Martin Colyer

F Reader's Digest

Jonathan Cusick
Desert Island
Disks - Brian May

M Acrylic

B To show the Queen
   guitarist on a desert
   island playing his
   distinctive 'red
   special', which he
   chose as a luxury item

C Sara Ramsbottom
F BBC Worldwide Ltd

Born to be Wild

M Acrylic

B A Radio 4 series
about eccentrics with
a passion for animals.
This first programme
featured a lady who
monitored adders,
recognising named
individuals

Good Eggs All

M Acrylic

B Caricatures of
TV characters
considered 'good
eggs', part of an
advertorial for Lion
Quality Eggs

C Sara Ramsbottom

F BBC Worldwide Ltd

C Daniel Coupe

F BBC Worldwide Ltd

Cyrus Deboo
SMS Bird

M Digital

B To illustrate a cover
supplement on mobile
communications
and SMS marketing

C Sinead Moriarty

F Precision Marketing

Cyrus Deboo
Alcohol Abuse

M Digital

B To illustrate an article
about the effects of
alcohol abuse among
young women

Nick Dewar
French Wine

M Acrylic

B Famous for
plundering the
great artworks
of Europe, this
illustration had
to make clear that
the Germans had
done the same
with French wine

C Sarah Prescott

F You Magazine

C Sara Ramsbottom

F Radio Times

RadioTimes

Philip Disley
...and pigs might fry

M Mixed media

B A piece about a
Mississippi style
pig roast, where the
pig looked uncannily
like John Prescott

C Graham Black

F Financial Times

Jovan Djordjevic
Inside the Signal Box
M Digital
B Cricket umpires and
their gestures 2003

C Derek Balment
F The Guardian

Sarah Dyer
Little Black Dress

M Mixed media

B To illustrate a
humorous view on
the timeless classic -
'the little black
dress' - and its
different meanings
for every woman

Max Ellis
Preying for War

M Digital

B Who are the British
Hawks? 'We know
who's against war
with Iraq. But who
is for it?'

C Sara Ramsbottom

F Radio Times

C Fraser Mc Dermott

F The Guardian

Max Ellis

Segontium

M Digital

B Produce an accurate 'swim through' of the wreck of the Segontium from diver John Liddiard's site drawings

Byron

M Digital

B Produce a contemporary portrait of Byron to accompany a new 'intimate' biography

C Tami Levinson

F Diver Group

C Roger Browning

F The Guardian

Jason Ford
Honesty / Test

M Gouache

B To accompany
   a cross-Europe
   honesty poll

Andrew Foster
Human Touch

M Digital

B To communicate that
   speaking and touch
   help plants to grow

C Martin Colyer

F Reader's Digest

C Sara Ramsbottom

F Radio Times

James Fryer

Torture

M Acrylic

B To illustrate a person
bound and gagged
and about to be
tortured

The Dawn of
a New Era

M Acrylic

B To illustrate the
famous 'Dawn of Man'
scene from '2001
A Space Odyssey'
replacing the black
monolith with a
mobile phone

C Graeme James

F The Economist

C Penny Garrett

F The Economist

James Fryer

Defender of the Ethos

M Acrylic

B The Catholic church
must stand by and
help the promotion
of Catholic schools
and education

Rogue States

M Acrylic

B A survey of America
to illustrate rogue
states and the
threat they pose to
the Western world

C Steve Place

F The Scottish
Times Educational
Supplement

C Una Corrigan

F The Economist

Small is the New Big

M Acrylic

B Internet start-up
companies used
to be huge. Now
they are small and
consistent and
reaping the rewards

Bad Cover
for a Rainy Day

M Acrylic

B The insurance
industry is in poor
shape and that's
bad news for
policy holders

C Martin Parfitt

F Future Publishing

C Una Corrigan

F The Economist

Carolyn Gowdy
'All the Birds of the Air'

M Mixed media

B When an anorexic
teenage girl goes
missing, her family
and friends have their
own views on what
made her do it

Adam Graff
The Oldest
Swindlers in Town

M Mixed media

B To accompany an
editorial piece on
fraudulent pensioners
who have been
found to be on
the fiddle with their
housing benefit

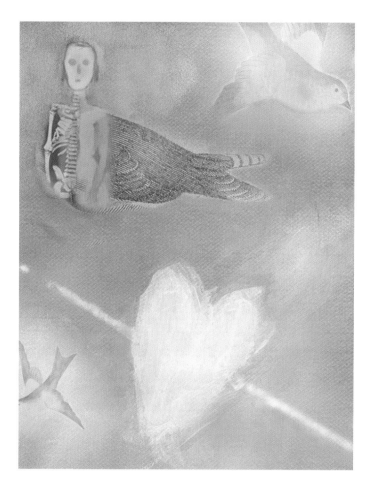

C Alex Nicholas
F Radio Times /
BBC Worldwide

C John Farley
F Daily Telegraph

Geoff Grandfield

Metropolis

M Pastel

B A radio dramatisation
of Fritz Lang's
stunning movie M.
The commission
had to reflect a
city living in fear

C Sara Ramsbottom

F Radio Times

RadioTimes

Matt Herring

	Company Mergers		Big Brother
M	Digital	**M**	Digital
B	The piece focused on company mergers and the behind the scenes deals and back stabbing that are common place. I used the analogy of a sinister dancing partnership who are not quite in step with one another	**B**	The piece focused on how some companies and government agencies have access to your email accounts and address books. A new government bill is due to be passed giving 'Big Brother' style legitimacy to this type of snooping

C	Alex Westthorpe
F	Computer Shopper

Peter Horridge
Shakespeare Portrait

M Pen, ink & digital,
Photoshop

B Produce a portrait
of Shakespeare
in your calligraphic
style incorporating
a passage by
The Bard to head
a magazine article

C Chris Parker

F John Brown Publishing

Frazer Hudson
Buying to Let
M Digital
B Create a playful
concept illustration
which encapsulates
the idea of looking
for and obtaining
properties to let

C James Dewar
F MDA
Communications

A Parent to
Two Generations

M Digital

B The illustration
must capture the
dual role of mothers
acting as parents
to two generations

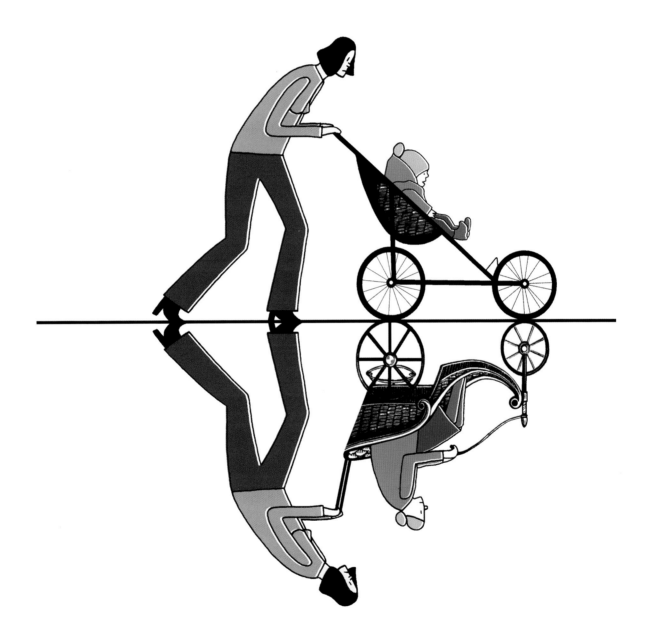

C Suzanne Davies

F The Mail on Sunday

David Humphries
Curriculum Pipeline

M Digital

B Depict the 'curriculum
   pipeline' - another
   new initiative to
   radically improve the
   teaching profession.
   The author suspects
   that it will have little
   effect

C Steve Place

F TES

Back to the Fuschia

M Digital

B Illustrate an article
about plants
becoming an integral
part of office design

Cactus Chair

M Digital

B Illustrate an article
about plants
becoming an integral
part of office design

C Sam Franks

F ETP Ltd

C Sam Franks

F ETP Ltd

Rod Hunt

European Homes

M Digital

B Illustrate the
differences between
homes around Europe;
homes furnished
using IKEA furniture

Atomic Robot

M Digital

B Illustrate an article
on Appleworks 6
software and how
it is perceived
to be uninspiring

C Martin Cotteral

F Cabal
Communications –
Ikea Room Magazine

C Jason Simmons

F Dennis Publishing -
MacUser

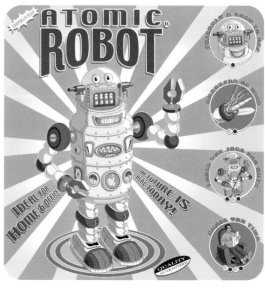

Adrian Johnson
How to be Glum

M Mixed Media

B To illustrate one of the
'how to ...' articles by
Guy Browning in the
'Weekend' magazine

C Maggie Murphy

F The Guardian

Satoshi Kambayashi

Stage Presence		Food and Ageing
M Digital		**M** Digital
B If you are going to engage your audience, you first need to define your own presence. Don't withdraw into your own little world		**B** What's the secret diet to keep fit and youthful when getting older?

C Jennifer Atigolo

F The Strad

C Sara Ramsbottom

F Radio Times

Under-age drinking

M Pen and ink
(line and wash)

B Relaxing licencing
laws will back-fire
as more and more
youngsters will get
hooked on drinking as
it happened in Ireland

Palestine's
Own Problem

M Pen and ink
(line and wash)

B What is less
highlighted about
the problems in the
Middle East is that
Palestinians are not
as united as people
assume

C Mike Topp

F The Guardian

C Mike Topp

F The Guardian

Matt Lee
Diary of an
F.D. in Trouble

M Mixed media

B To accompany
the diary of a
financial director
as his company
faces going under

July 5.

July 16.

August 2.

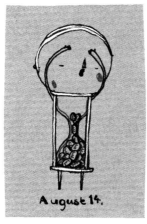

August 14.

September 17.

October 7.

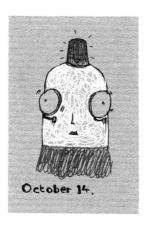

October 14.

October 22.

November 11.

C Rachel James

F Caspian Publishing

Sean Lee
Rowan Atkinson
Caricature

M Gouache

B Caricature of
Rowan Atkinson
as Blackadder for
a regular item about
a TV personality
or programme

C Caroline Sallis
F Radio Times

RadioTimes

Toby Leigh
Arcade Obsession
M Pen and ink (line
and wash) and digital
B Illustrate the
obsessive game
playing of yester-year

C Terry Stokes
F Edge Magazine

Frank Love
Layman on the Board
M   Mixed media
B   To depict the
actuality of having
a non-executive on
a board of governors

C   Dennis Sterne
F   EMAP Healthcare

Warren Madill
Michael Palin

M Acrylic

B One of a series
of paintings to
illustrate 'TV's
national treasures'.
Here, Michael Palin
is portrayed as
the Mona Lisa with
elements of his
TV work in the
background

Daniel Marcolin
Middlesex

M Mixed media

B Illustration for 'Mixte'
magazine - article
about the author
Jeffrey Eugenides
and his book
'Middlesex' about a
main character, part
boy, part girl, a male
hermaphrodite

C Paul Smith

F Radio Times

C Cécile Alizon

F Mixte September
2003 issue

Angel

M Mixed media

B Article about failure
in the French audio-
visual field today

Debra McFarlane

The Ideal Heroine

M Etching & aquatint

B The novelist Henry
James threw piles
of dresses that had
belonged to his dead
friend Constance
Fenimore Woolson
into a Venetian lagoon
to 'drown' them

C Cecile Alizon

F Mixte Feb-March
2003 issue

C Sara Ramsbottom

F Radio Times

Belle Mellor

Salmon Man

M Pen and ink / digital

B For an article about
the creation of
a new fabric made
from salmon skin

Scam

M Pen and ink

B For an article on car
mechanics who rip
off elderly customers

C Jane Moss

F Director Magazine

C Courtney Murphy
Price

F Segunda Juventud

Grindstone

M Pen and ink / digital

B For a quote about
the elderly having
to work for longer
before retirement

Sumo

M Pen and ink / digital

B To illustrate a quote by
a broadsheet editor
saying that competing
against Murdoch's
newspapers is like
waking up with
a Sumo wrestler

Word Count

M Pen and ink

B An article which tallies
the number of words
Shakespeare created

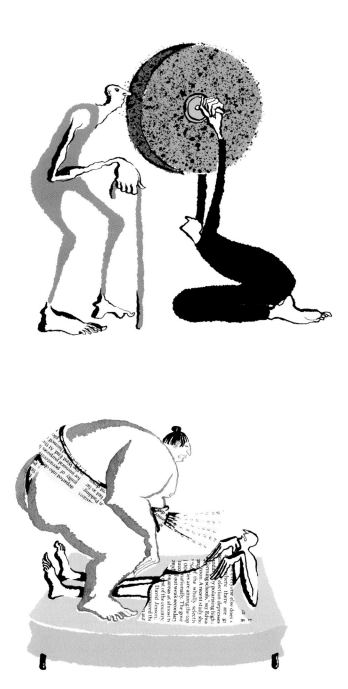

C Jane Moss

F Director Magazine

C Jane Moss

F Director Magazine

C Nick Robins

F Shakespeare's Globe

Tom Morgan - Jones
Tricolor Trouble

M Ink & digital

B The French ship the
Tricolor containing
70,000 tons of
gas-oil capsized.
It was then struck
by two ships on two
separate occasions

Gunnlaug Moen Hembery
In the Fast Food Lane

M Mixed media

B Illustration about
the changes in food
habits, and how it
affects us physically
and psychologically

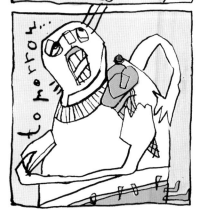

C Toby Venables

F Odd Hack Publishing

C Gudleiv Forr

F Dagbladet

Steven O'Brien

Travelling With
Your Boss

M Ink & digital

B To accompany
a piece on the
awkwardness
of spending
many hours close
to the boss on
business trips

Will OPCE Out
the Flow of Oil

M Ink & digital

B Oil sheiks trying
to cut the supply

C Olga Rapaport

F The New York Times

C Merryn Somerset
Webb

F Dennis Publishing

Mark Oldroyd
Peace In Our Time
M Acrylic
B Poet Louis Macneice is pictured within a backdrop of Neville Chamberlain, an image to match a reading of Macneice's poem on the end of love and peace

Dettmer Otto
Imagination
M Digital
B Free brief to theme of imagination, cover illustration

Paquebot
Dog Racism
M Digital
B To accompany an article asking - 'Can dogs be racist?'

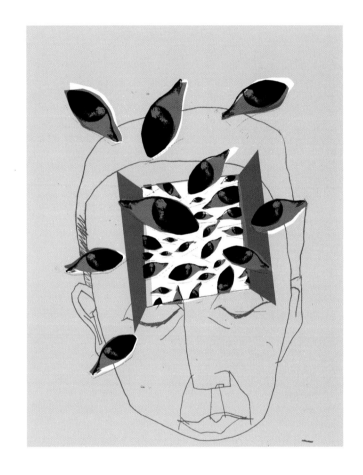

C Sara Ramsbottom
F Radio Times

C Gabriel Solomons
F Decode Magazine

C Martin Colyer
F Reader's Digest

RadioTimes

Simon Pemberton
One Careful Owner

M   Mixed media

B   To depict the strange
    sub culture of people
    who live, work and
    earn a living in virtual
    on-line gaming
    worlds by collecting
    and selling game
    related 'treasures'

C   Craig Mackie

F   New Scientist

Ian Pollock
Portrait of
Cyril Connolly

M Watercolour / ink
B Portrait of Cyril
Connolly for Guardian
Review cover
C Roger Browning
F The Guardian

Matthew Richardson
The Lovely Bones

M Mixed media

B To illustrate Alice
Seebold's surreal
novel, 'The Lovely
Bones' which
describes a girls
murder, her life in
heaven and her
ongoing effect
on the living

C Sharron Morgan

F The Times

Chris Robson
History of Apple
Timeline

M   Digital

B   Three double page
spreads covering
the people and
development of Apple
Computers (research
nightmare-a-thon)

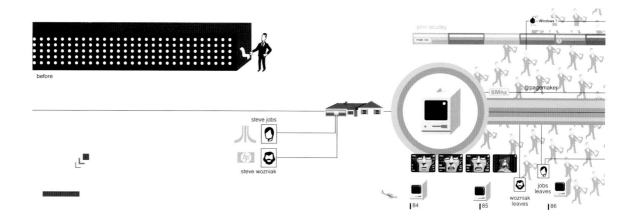

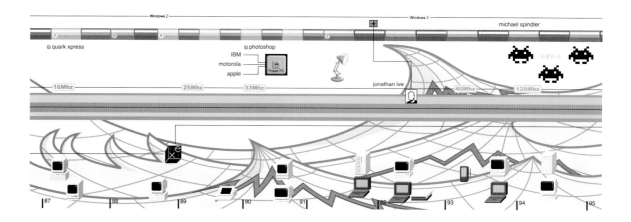

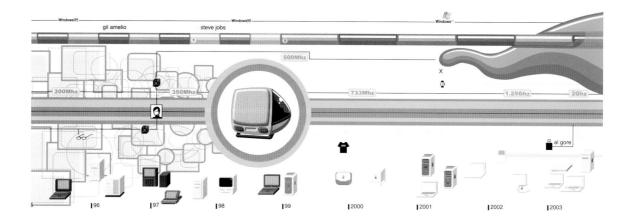

C   Jason Simmons

F   Dennis Publishing

Michael Sheehy
Television Violence

M Mixed media

B How violence
on TV can affect
the behaviour of
younger viewers

Harriet Russell
Personal Growth

M Collage, pen
& screen print

B Image to illustrate an
article named 'making
room for growth'
about the benifits of
reiki and counselling
in the stressful
modern world

C Sara Ramsbottom

F Radio Times

C Anamaria Stanley

F Time Out

Lasse Skarbovik
Astro Challenge

M   Digital

B   One page illustration
for Glamour Magazine
about astrology

Paul Slater
Murder

M   Acrylic

B   A murder mystery -
or is it? Dark humour
is at work as a group
of friends start
dropping like flies
on a weekend away

Shakespeare
in the Dock

M   Acrylic

B   Illustration
accompanying
feature on
'Shakespeare in
the dock' examining
the legacy and
relevance left behind
by Shakespeare
portrayed as a
rebellious character

C   Geoff Waring

F   Glamour Magazine

C   Caroline Sallis

F   Radio Times

C   Paul Smith

F   Radio Times

RadioTimes   RadioTimes

Jonathan Ross

M Acrylic

B One of a series
of paintings to
illustrate 'TV's
national treasures'.
Based on a famous
painting, Jonathan
Ross' demeanour
is captured with
a pastiche of
Gainsborough's
Blue Boy

C Paul Smith

F Radio Times

RadioTimes

Josephine Sumner
The Size of
Things to Come?
M   Scraperboard / digital
B   To show robots
    building progressively
    smaller robots
    thereby illustrating
    nanotechnology

C   Frank Foster
F   Haymarket Publishing

David Tazzyman
Yoga

M   Mixed media

B   To illustrate a
minimalist and
fashionable
London apartment

F   Red Wood

**Tobatron
(Toby Leigh)**
Future Environments
M Digital
B Illustrate the
building site, office
and apartment
of the future

Nancy Tolford
Highbrow
M Digital
B Article about how
skilled eyebrow
grooming can
completely transform
one's appearance

Bob Venables
Grand Odalisque
M Alkyd
B Illustration to show
how TV stars of today
will remain classics
for the future

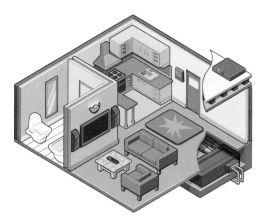

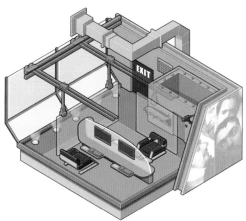

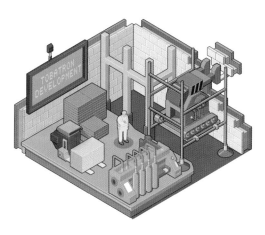

C Joe Presedo
F Building 160

C Graham Ball
F The Times

C Paul Smith
F Radio Times

Jane Webster
Sociable Soho
M Pencil
B Draw a night in Soho
for 'Talk of the Town'
Magazine, Sunday
Independent

Stefano Vitale
Ginny Grows Up
M Oil paint on wood
B An article about a
woman who, although
she has the mental
age of a child, shows
her foster family her
courage

C Caroline Roberts
F Independent

C Martin Colyer
F Reader's Digest

Chris West
David Jason

M Acrylic

B One of a series
of paintings to
illustrate 'TV's
national treasures'.
Here, David Jason
has been recreated
appropriately as the
laughing cavalier

C Paul Smith

F Radio Times

RadioTimes

Ian Whadcock
Things To Do When
You're Dead

M Digital

B To show how your
body can be used in
unusual ways if you
donate it to Science
when you die. In this
case your body is left
to decompose in a
field to aid forensic
research

Snooze Control

M Digital

B A column on the
discomfort of
sleeping in cars.
Memory of cold
nights & lack of
sleep trying to get
comfortable in your
average family car

C John-Henry Barac

F The Guardian

C Peter Charles

F Forward Group

Jonathan Williams
Things You
Shouldn't Do After
the Age of 30
M   Pencil / Photoshop
B   Part 12: Own an item
of clothing by Kangol

C   Craig Lancaster
F   National Magazines

Jonathan Williams
A Closer Look at
Ecological Sanitation
M Pencil / Photoshop
B Delegates at
the international
conference on
eco-sanitation in
Nanning peer down
a two-ended urine
diverting toilet

Biker Chef at the
Embassy Hotel
M Pencil / Photoshop
B A portrait of Garry
Hollihead, the mean
and the moody chef
who rides a Harley
between the Embassy
and the Marquee

Lee Woodgate
Alan Partridge
M Digital
B A portrait of Alan
Partridge for a piece
written for TimeOut

C Dinyar Godrej
F New Internationalist

C Claire Hayter
F Restaurant

C Sandy Suffield
F TimeOut London

Philip Wrigglesworth
Out For Good

M Mixed media

B To illustrate the
problem inmates
face when returning
into society with no
money, no address
and a criminal record

C Garry Burton

F Big Issue in the North

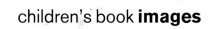

Children's books
Gold award winner

Julie Monks
Foot Prints

M Oils

B To create illustrations
for a children's book

C Caroline Gott

F Scholastic Ltd.

Stephanie Alexander

Hector the Balloon
Collector

M Collage

B I was commissioned
to illustrate five stories
for a programme on
CITV called 'Ripley
and Scuff'. Images
came up on screen
while 'Story Princess'
read the story out

Hector the
Leaf Collector

M Collage

B I was commissioned
to illustrate five stories
for a programme on
CITV called 'Ripley
and Scuff'. Images
came up on screen
while 'Story Princess'
read the story out

Michael Bramman

The Princesses
of Bamar

M Acrylic

B Show the two
princesses
descending a spiral
staircase with fantasy
forest and towers

C Susan Anderton

F The Childrens
Company

C Frank Niedertubbesing

F INIT GmbH for
C. Bertelsmann
Verlag München

Sarah Dyer
Clementine & Mungo
M Mixed media
B Double page spread
for a book about
Mungo who asks
a lot of questions
and Clementine who
seems to know all the
right answers until…

Children's books
Bronze award winner

Sara Fanelli
First Flight
M Collage
B Butterfly flies to China

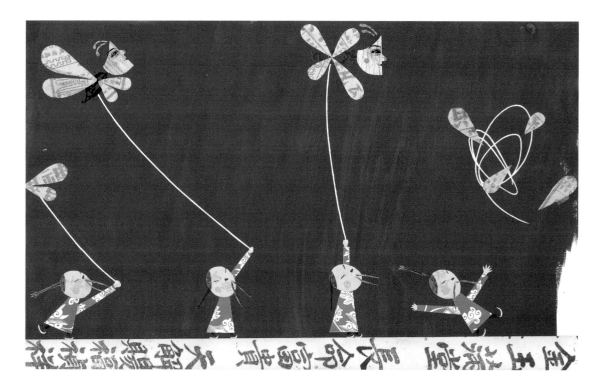

C Sarah Odedina
F Bloomsbury

C Jonathan Cape
F Random House
Children's Books

Sarah Gill
The Truffle Hunt
M Gouache & ink
B To illustrate a story
about a truffle hunt

Suzanna Hubbard

The Lady Who
Lived in a Car (2)

M Watercolour

B I wrote and illustrated
a picture book
influenced by a real
lady who lived in a car

The Lady Who
Lived in a Car (1)

M Watercolour

B 'And Miss Lettuce
told the best stories
ever!' A spread
from The Lady Who
Lived in a Car

C Liz Flanagan

F Chrysalis Books Plc

Sarah Mc Menemy
Jack's New Boat

M Mixed media

B Author/illustrator

C Denise Johnstone-Burt

F Walker Books

Julie Monks

More Precious than Gold

M Oils

B To illustrate a children's story by Gillian Lobel

Winter Magic

M Oils

B To illustrate a book for children

C Kate Burns

F Hodder Children's Books

C Caroline Gott

F Scholastic Ltd.

Lydia Monks

Crocodile

M Mixed media

B 'She tried playing
Snap! with a crocodile,
but it just couldn't
shuffle and she
didn't like his smile'

Monkeys

M Mixed media

B To illustrate the
endpapers for the
book 'The Skipping
Rope Snake'

Tom Morgan-Jones

Le Renard

M Ink & digital

B Jacket to entice
children aged 5-7
to learn French

C Alison Green

F Macmillan

C Zuza Vrbova

F Red Zebra

Garry Parsons
The Four Franks

M Acrylic

Children's books
Silver award winner

B Frank has lost the ship given to him by his Great Grandpa

C Mandy Norman

F Egmont Books

Sarah Perkins
Three Blind Eyes
M   Mixed media
B   The story of a young
girl caught up in the
terrifying underworld
of Victorian London

C   Donna Thynne
F   Oxford University
Press

Susan Scott
Puss in Boots
M Colour pencil
B Cover artwork for
children's picture
book about the
adventures of the
social climbing cat
in Charles Perrault's
fairy tale, to be
published by
Templar, 2004

Bee Willey
Wooden Dragon 2
M Digital
B Handle sets off to
sea on a long journey

C Mandy Wood
F Templar Publishing

C Ian Craig /
Delia Huddy
F Random House
Children's Books

Stephen Waterhouse

'Then they
go fishing…!'

M   Acrylic

B   To write and illustrate
a sequel to 'Get Busy
this Christmas'

'Soon they fall fast
asleep under the
twinkling stars'

M   Acrylic

B   To write and illustrate
a sequel to 'Get
Busy this Christmas'

'And cook the
tasty fish on a
HOT barbecue!'

M   Acrylic

B   To write and illustrate
a sequel to 'Get
Busy this Christmas'

C   Emma Matthewson

F   Bloomsbury
Children's Books

Anne Wilson
On the Savannah
M   Mixed media
B   'African Princess'
     – a full colour
     children's picture
     book highlighting
     cultural diversity
     for young children

C   Penny Walker
F   Random House

Counting the Days

M Mixed media

Christopher Wormell
Two Frogs

M Watercolour

B Author/Illustrator

C Tom Maschler

F Random House
Children's Books

Books
Gold award winner

Lasse Skarbovik
The Curious
Incident of the Dog
in the Night-time

M Digital

B A story about
an autistic boy

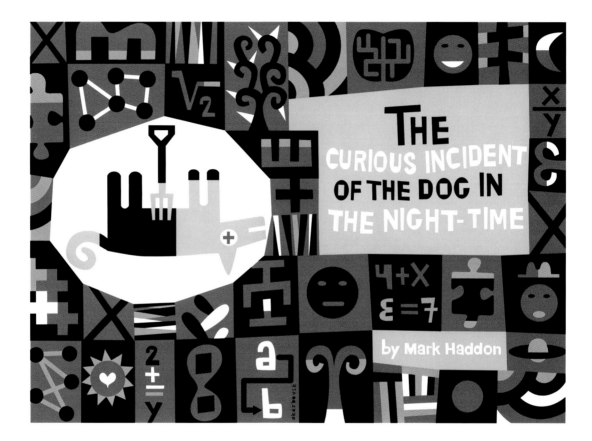

C Conorde Clarke
F Reader's Digest

Katherine Baxter
Tudor House
M Watercolour
B Book of 17 double
page spreads - cross-
section cutaways
of houses starting
from the cave to
a futuristic home

A. Richard Allen
The Loved One
M Ink & digital
B Book jacket for
edition of Evelyn
Waugh's 'The
Loved One'

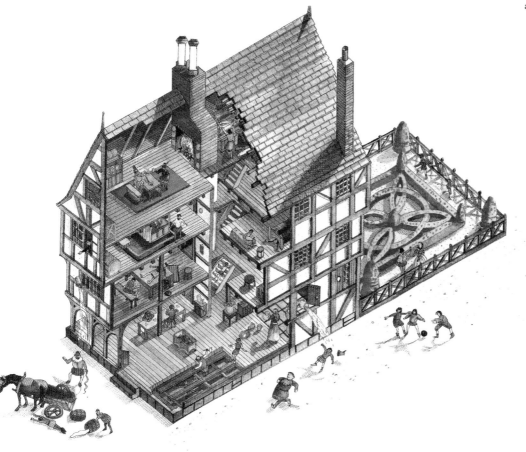

C Sarah Nunn
F BBC Worldwide
Publishing

C Roman Milisic
F Freelance Art Director

Russell Cobb
The ABC of
Behaviour
M Acrylic
B To produce a
series of 6 book
covers produced
as educational
teaching aids.
The book deals with
classroom behaviour
management

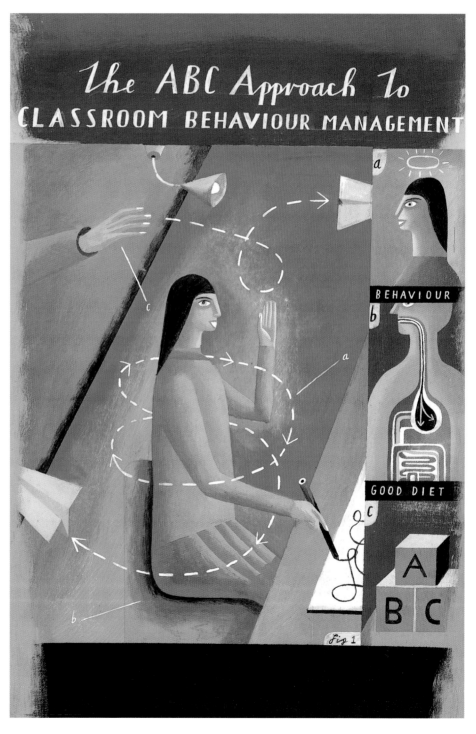

C Murray Marshall
F Lifetime Careers
Publishing

Sarah Gibb
My Fat Brother
M Watercolour & ink
B Book jacket

C John Hamilton
F Penguin Books

Willi Gray

The Arabian
Nightmare

M Mixed media

B Arabian nights-style
fantasy by Robert
Irwin. A meditation
on reality and illusion
through the affliction
of the Arabian
Nightmare: an
unrecollectable
dream of infinite
suffering

The Others

M Drawing,
digital collage

B The Others by Xavier
Garcia Sanchez.
A psychological
ghost story about
the phenomenon of
disappeared people
and the watchers that
can see them

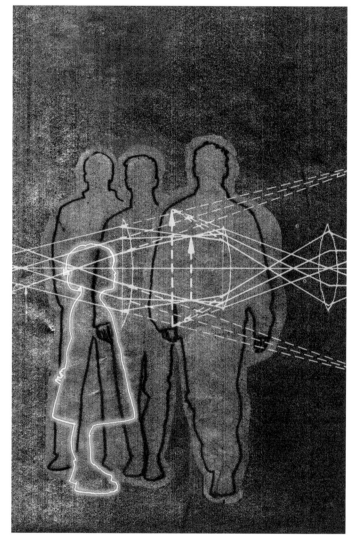

C Eric Lane

F Dedalus Publishing

Nick Hardcastle
The Thirty-Nine Steps

M Pen and ink (the
colour was obtained
using ink overlays)

B To produce a image
which shows the hero
escaping from his
pursuers. The image
could only employ
a limited number of
colours and not too
much detail

C Joe Whitlock-Blundell

F Folio Society

Matt Herring

Lucky

M Digital

B Design a cover
to run with Eddie
de Oliveira's comic
drama about a young
man's sexuality crisis
& the love triangle
between the 3 main
characters. The cover
focuses on their trip
to the London Eye
& London Aquarium

Where Were
You Robert?

M Digital

B Design a cover about
the 15 year old boy,
Robert, who travels
through time and
space to different
events in history. One
minute he's in 18th
century Holland with
windmills, the next in
the Australian outback

Rian Hughes
His dark materials
trilogy, Northern
Lights, The Subtle
Knife, The Amber
Spyglass

M   Digital

B   Compact disc sleeve
cover images for
the three books
in Philip Pullman's
acclaimed trilogy,
his dark materials

C   Matt Bookman

F   BBC Audiobooks

 Audiobooks

Peter Jones
North Carr Lightship
M Watercolour
B Personal work -
one of a series of
illustrations for a
book on lighthouses
of Scotland

Leonie Lord
The Charge of
the Light Brigade
M Digital
B To illustrate the
atmosphere and
sounds of the poem

C Appletree Press
F Northern Lighthouse
Board

C Sirida Pensri
F Harcourt Books

Richard Lyon
Citizenship

M Pastel

B Illustrate the
relationship
between the citizen,
the political process,
the community and
the state

Peter Malone
Opera Stories /
Die Fledermaus

M Gouache

B To illustrate a
book on opera

C Amina Dudhia

F Hodder & Stoughton

C Christine Carswell

F Chronicle Books

Debra McFarlane
'Dinner at
San Salvatore'

M Etching & aquatint

B To illustrate the novel
'The Enchanted April'
by Elizabeth Von
Arnhim, which is set
in a castle in Italy
in the early 1920's

Mark Oldroyd
The Falls

M Acrylic

B Create atmospheric
piece to echo the
tone of the book

Books
Bronze award winner

Nigel Owen
Clear Waters Rising

M Digital

B To illustrate an
account of a journey
on foot from western
Spain to Istanbul

C Joe Whitlock Blundell

F The Folio Society

C Andrew Hall

F BBC Audiobooks

C Andrew Smith

F Penguin

BBC Audiobooks

Sarah Perkins

Firedrakes's Eye

M Mixed media

B An Elizabethan tale of
murder and treason -
set against the filthy
crowded splendour of
16th Century London

C Patrick Carpenter

F Orion Publishing

Books
Silver award winner

Paul Rogers

Bix Beiderbecke
for Jazz ABC

M Acrylic

B Illustrations for a book
on 26 Jazz legends

Lester Young
for Jazz ABC

M Acrylic

B Illustrations for a book
on 26 Jazz legends

C Chris Paul

F Candlewick Press

C Chris Paul

F Candlewick Press

Rachel Ross
Dr Finlay - Further
Adventures
of a Black Bag
M   Acrylic
B   Cassette & CD
illustration for
Radio 4's Dr Finlay -
Further Adventures
of a Black Bag

Bill Sanderson
Old Curiosity Shop
M   Coloured inks
B   Audio cassette
sleeve cover image
of Charles Dickens'
famous novel

C   Andrew Hall
F   BBC Audiobooks

C   Matt Bookman
F   BBC Audiobooks

BBC Audiobooks

BBC Audiobooks

Peter Warner
The Cats of
Moon Cottage
by Marilyn Edwards

M Watercolour

B Loose, expressive
jacket design
reduced to simplest
elements evoking
the mysterious,
beguiling relationship
between an old
resident cat and
a young newcomer

C Patrick Knowles

F Hodder &
Stoughton Ltd

To Begin With
He Ignores Her

M Pencil

B One of 70 loose,
spontaneous
drawings capturing
felinity to illustrate
a poignant true story
of the beguiling
of independent old
Septi by young Otto

Ian Whadcock
Audio Book
Collection

M Digital

B To create a cover
image showing how
BBC Audio products
can be incorporated
into your daily routine
at home - down the
gym or on the move

C Matt Bookman
F BBC Audiobooks

B B C Audiobooks

Student
Gold award winner

Sharon Tancredi
The Wolf and
Seven Kids

M   Digital

B   Grimm fairytale
adapted to
an A1 poster

Paul Allison
Ollie, Why
Don't I Feel Well?

M Watercolour

B Children's picture
book, entered for
Macmillan Children's
Book Prize 2003 -
highly commended

Beth Louella Aulton

African Boy

M Mixed media

B To create an image
for a magazine
article on quotations

'Rub Those
Scribbles Out'

M Mixed media

B To write and illustrate
a children's picture
book - (12 double
page spreads)

"GO AND GET A RUBBER AND
RUB THOSE SCRIBBLES OUT!"

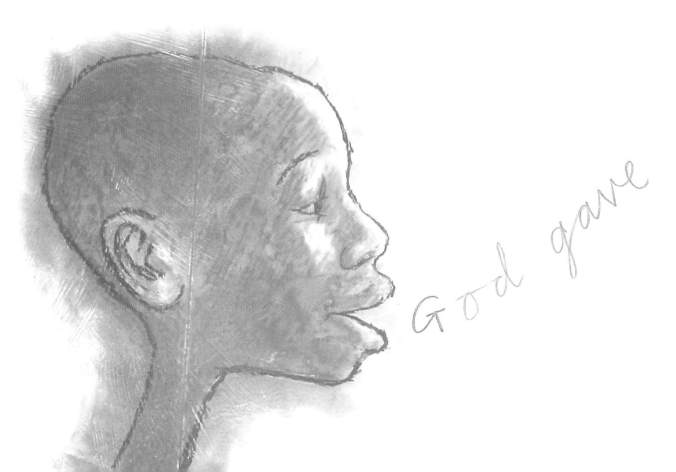

Emma Baker

Moment in Time

M Cotton thread hand
stitched on to calico

B To produce a
self-indulgent
piece of work that
demonstrates my
interests, to be
used for my degree
show exhibition

Ed Barnes
Little Red
Riding Hood

M   Linocut print

B   Revamping and
reinventing old
nursery rhymes/fairy
tales for the new
generation
of youngsters

Ian Benfold Haywood
Summertime

M   Mixed media

B   To capture the mood
and atmosphere of
a traditional British
seaside resort

Dawn Bishop
England
M Mixed media
B People and
their cultures

Michael Cadd
Lifestyle Illustration
M Mixed Media
B To produce a
lifestyle illustration
that reflects my
autographic style
and interest in
fashion illustration

Clémence de Limburg
Flamencat
M China ink & digital
screenprint
B Flamenco poster

Jane Donald
Mr Daddy Longlegs
and Mr Floppy Fly

M Photo-montage

B To re-illustrate a
nonsense poem/story
by Edward Lear,
minimum of 8pps and
front and back covers

Ben Farnell
Shedding Light

M Mixed media

B Editorial illustration
for an article about
artists attempts at
tackling the subject
of homelessness

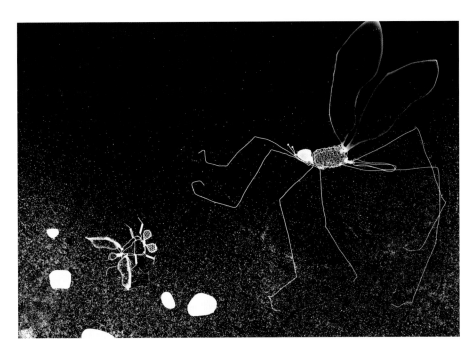

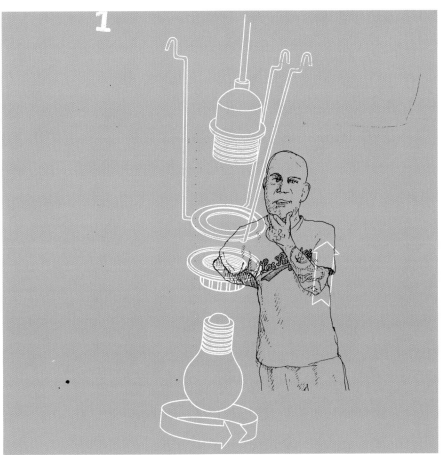

Philip Grisewood
Big Mac
M Mixed media
B To produce an
   anti-MacDonalds
   protest poster

Kayo Harada

The Folk of the
Faraway Tree

M Mixed media

B The image from
the children's book
'The Folk of the
Faraway Tree' and
my imagination

Ben Hawkes

Hearing Voices

M Collage

B To illustrate
the schizophrenic
experience of
hearing voices
(audio hallucinations)

The Goon Show

M Collage

B To produce an
illustration that
summarises and
encapsulates the
old radio show 'The
Goon Show', focuses
on the feel and
humour of the show

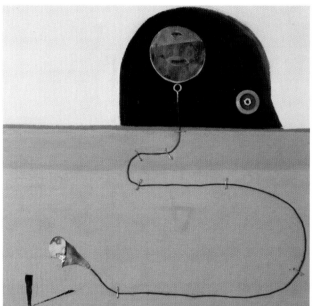

Eva-Kajsa Hedström
Queue 2
M Digital
B One out of 3 images
created for an article
on queuing in London

Sarah Howe
Tapas

M Printmaking & collage

B An illustration to
accompany an article
about Spanish cuisine

Michelle MacRae

Reflection

M Paint, inks, tissue paper & newspaper

B This image was inspired by Night Poem, by Margaret Atwood, and is one of a set of 12 images produced for a series of books

Sitting Chick

M Digital

B This image was inspired by Chicken Licken by Maya Angelou and is one of a set of eight images produced for a series of books.

Mei Matsuoka

Cancer	Co-operation	Do We Really
M Collage	**M** Mixed media	Need Men?
B Editorial illustration	**B** Personal work	**M** Collage
for Cancer Research	developed to be used	**B** To illustrate an article
	in an editorial context	regarding the growing
		concern over science
		enabling women to
		reproduce without
		the need for men

Sarah Nelson

The Cement Garden

M Mixed media

B Book jacket image
for the novel by
Ian McEwan

Oranges Are Not
the Only Fruit

M Mixed media

B Book jacket image
for the novel by
Jeanette Winterson

Lisa Raftery
Funsplash

M Mixed media

B Part of a set of
four posters to
advertise Butlins
Holiday Camps

Erika Richmond
Vintage

M Mixed media

B Create a stand-up
in-store image as
promotional material
for 'vintage' retro
clothes label. Models
to have non-descript
clothes on but still be
promoting fashion

Rosie Scott
Surprise

M Oil paint & Photoshop

B Produce a sequence
that contains surprise

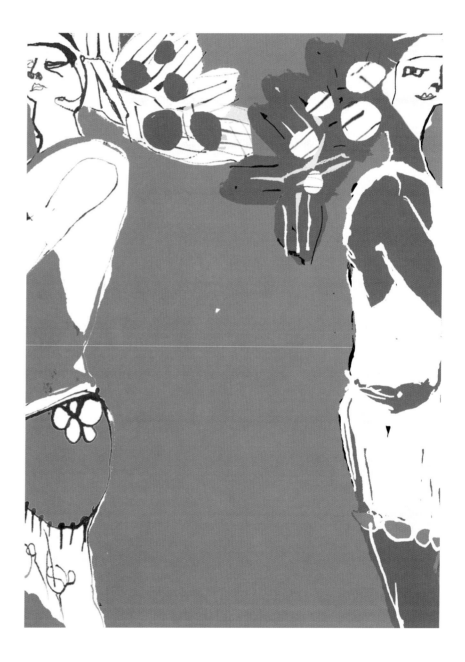

Lucie Sheridan
Hybrids
M Gouache
B Self promotion

Mark Slack
Storyboard of
title sequence
to 'The Goonies'

M Digital

B To create an
animated title
sequence for
the re-release
of Spielberg's
'The Goonies'

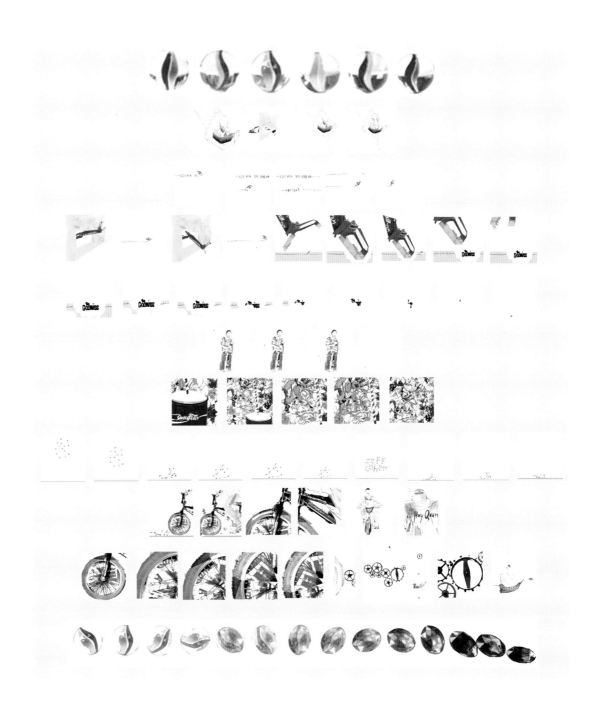

Benjamin Bogart Small
Fate Cards

M   Acrylic, bleach & ink

B   Set of cards to do
with fate - to promote
self as graduate

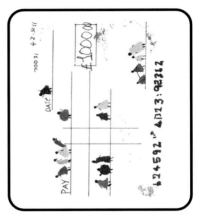

There is money
coming to you

you will be robbed
by a swine

you shall find a
new love

you will be caught in a
compromising position

there will be a promotion
opportunity at work

enjoy an excellent
meal

Phil Smith
Marks and Spencer

M Digital

B Illustration for
an article about
Marks and Spencer
underwear entitled
'Reasonable Prices
for a Reasonable
Nation'

Julia Staite
Bruce, aged 5

M Collage

B Page from an
illustrated book
based on comments
made by children,
this comment from
Nanette Newman's
book, 'God Bless Love'

Christina Stone
Winter Thoughts

M Ink (Indian & sepia)
& wax resist

B Write a piece of
narrative that is
personal to you.
Illustrate with 12
sequential illustrations
(7 x 9 cm) with one
line of narrative
to one image

Sharon Tancredi

Talking Turkeys

M Acrylic / Collage

B Image from a book
   of poems on the
   theme of animals

The Cow

M Acrylic / Collage

B Image from a book
   of poems on the
   theme of animals

192

Student
Bronze award winner

Naomi Tipping
Granny's Marbles (1)

M Mixed media

B To write and illustrate
a picture book aimed
at adults that takes
a humorous yet
sympathetic glance
at the difficulties
of ageing

Granny's Marbles (2)   Granny's Marbles (3)

Naomi Tipping

Insomnia

M Mixed media

B To illustrate an article
about insomnia

Flying with Bees

M Mixed media

B To illustrate Spike
Milligan's poem,
'Two Children (small)'
about a child wishing
to fly like the bees

Jago Titcomb
The White Snake

M Digital

B To illustrate a Grimm's
fairy tale in a bold,
colourful and
contemporary way

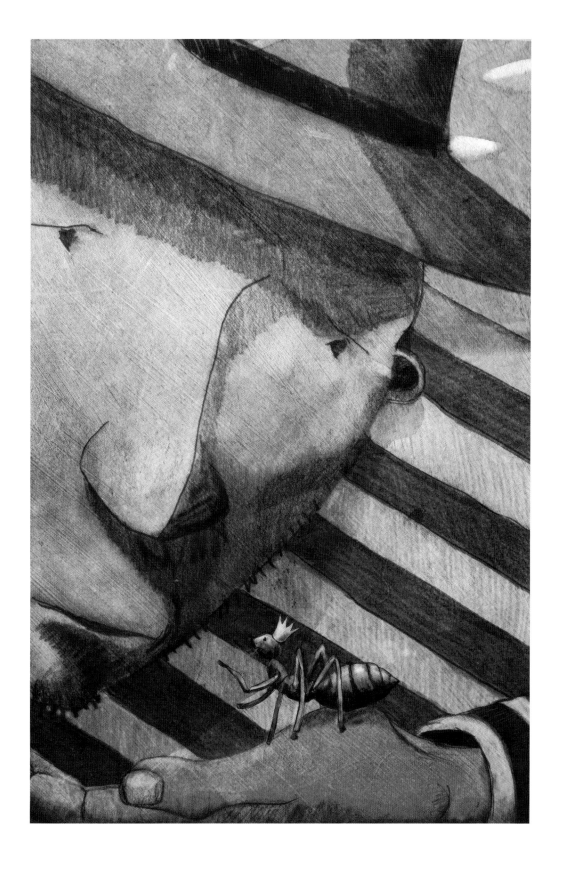

Corrin Tulk
Resin Babies
M Resin / photography
B 3D pieces for
   major project on
   vaccination damage

Helen Turner
'Out On The Prowl'
M Digital
B Produce a
   competition poster for
   'Dazed and Confused'
   magazine on a theme
   depicting "Beauty
   In The Street".
   My reference reveals
   animal instincts
   in urban Newcastle

'Bird' Watching

M   Digital

B   An illustration exercise
for 'Cosmopolitan'
magazine on the
romanticism of
outdoor sex to feature
in a story about a
couple's spontaneous
birdwatching
expedition!

Donat Willenz

Dawn Chorus

M Indian ink,
gouache, collage

B Asked to illustrate
8.06 am. I thought of
how we belong to a
network and respond
to grids and numbers
as opposed to…
birds for instance

La Douce Heure
du Diable

M Indian ink, Photoshop

B This image was
created for a calendar.
Each illustrator was
given a specific
month and asked to
illustrate its number,
in this case, 12
for December… or
midnight, the sweet
hour of the devil

Andy Smith
Eat Out
M Mixed media
B Eating out in London

Unpublished
Gold award winner

David Bimson

It's A London Thing

M Gouache / digital

B Self promotional

Gun Smuggling

M Gouache / digital

B Self initiated image
inspired by an article
highlighting recent
lapses in airport
security

Jan Bowman
Barman
Amsterdam 2003
M Digital
B From a series
of life sketches

Michael Bramman

South Beach

M Acrylic

B Print project

Reflection LA 1

M Acrylic

B Print project

Jo Brown
Shouting
M Gouache
B Self-promotional
illustration for
own book idea

Paul Brown
Child Abuse
M Mixed media
B Image dealing with
undoing the emotional
damage suffered by
the victims of abuse

Finn Campbell Notman

Peckham

M Digital

B London particulars

Dave Cavanagh

Rhinoceros and Bird

M Acrylic

B Illustration based
on the theme
of 'All Creatures
Great and Small

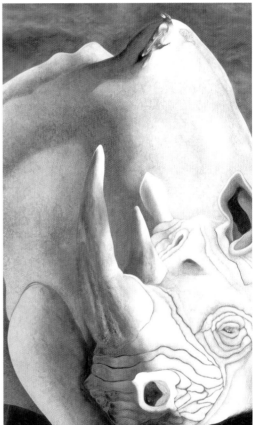

206

John Cei Douglas
From My Bed

M Watercolour

B From a 43 page
comic rough draft,
pondering the infinite
possibilities of what
you could do if, in fact,
you decided to stay
in bed and do nothing
at all; not limiting
yourself to going
and doing any one
particular thing

Scott Chambers

Z- Mail

M Mixed media

B Self promotional
piece looking
at the state of
the postal service

Poloroid King

M Mixed media

B Self promotional
piece looking
at male vanity

John Charlesworth
Tell-Tale (Part one) | Tell-Tale (Part two)

M Digital | **M** Digital

B The first in a series of two personal art works, reflecting upon the distortion of classical folk tales by the preconception of Hollywood ideology | **B** The second in a series of two personal art works, reflecting upon the distortion of classical folk tales by the preconception of Hollywood ideology

Nishant Choksi
Villainous

M Digital

B A series of self
   promotional
   postcards placing
   characters in
   situations of peril

Russell Cobb

The New Faces Works

M Acrylic

B To produce a series of
unique and collectable
postcards designed
to heighten awareness
of the illustrator's
work. No.30 based
on the theme of
unusual heads

The New
Theatre Works

M Acrylic

B To produce a series of
unique and collectable
postcards designed
to heighten awareness
of the illustrator's
work.No.33 based on
the theme of theatre

The New Woodworks

M Acrylic

B To produce a series of
unique and collectable
postcards designed
to heighten awareness
of the illustrator's
work. No.31 playing
on the idea of the
artist's work being
a handmade product

Nicky Cooney
Let Fly the Birds

M Collograph
and watercolour

B Illustration for
children's story

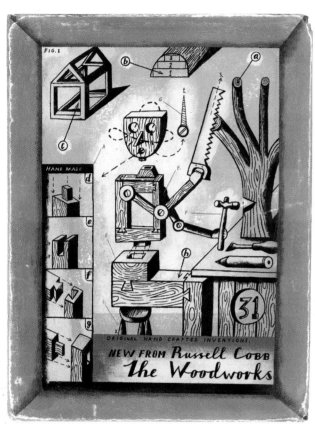

Jonathan Croft

PIG

M Mixed media

B Book cover for
the novel 'PIG'
by Andrew Cowan

The Buffalo
Roam Again

M Mixed media

B Editorial article -
the human population
of North Dakota
is moving on and
buffalo are returning
to the plains

Mel Croft

Eating Out by Bus,
Tube and River

M Mixed media

B To produce an
artwork, suitable for
use as a poster for
Transport For London,
with elements possible
for use as abstractions
for supporting
promotional material

Ian Dodds
Dream Job
M Digital
B Self-promotional
editorial piece that
followed city-slickers
leaving high paid
jobs to pursue their
dream careers

Stephen Elford
Results Day (10
Minutes Remaining)
M Mixed media
B Personal work -
character studies on
the theme of waiting

Kate Edmunds
Funny Farm
M Watercolour
B Illustration from a
children's book idea
called 'Funny Farm'

Johanna Fernihough
Flora

M   Photo-montage

B   To create an image
for Début Art's
Illumination
Exhibition 2003

Kirstie Fitzgerald
Victorian Traveller

M   Pencil

B   Personal piece - to be
used in promotional
literature context for
a Victorian museum:
represent the
character and appeal
of the museum using
a staff member

Rachel Goslin
The Graduate
M Mixed media
B Produce a speculative
mock-up book
cover for the novel
'The Graduate'

Vincent Gould
Other
M Mixed media
B To respond to an
article on racial
classification

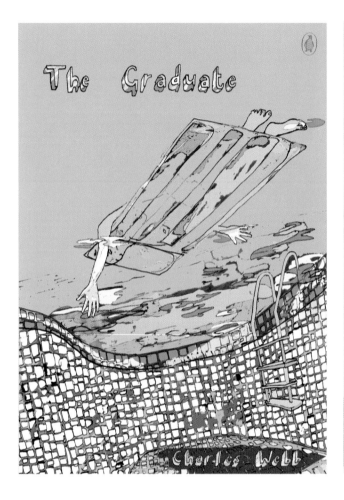

C Heike Rochau
F Sieger Design
for Ritzenhoff

Adam Graff
Ice Cream

M   Mixed media

B   Donated piece
generated for
charity 'Paintings
in Hospitals'

Peter Grundy
Headcase   Squareheads
M Digital
B Squareheads: A set
of six posters of life
made simple in words
and pictures

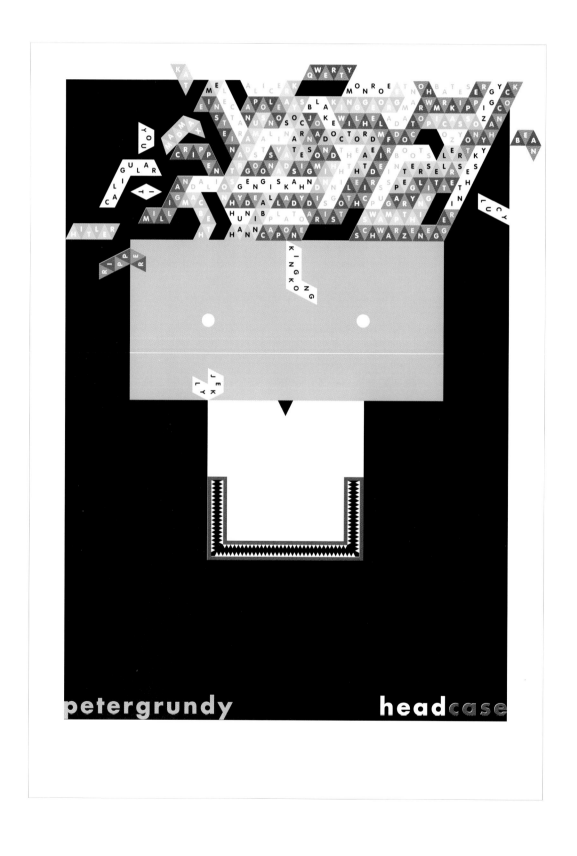

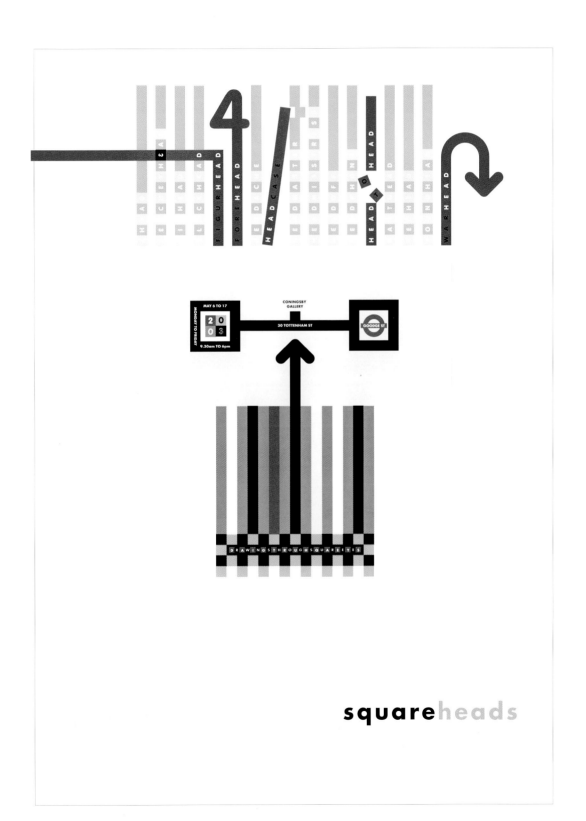

squareheads

Kevin Hauff
Rocket Commuter

M Acrylic, collage
& digital

B Experimental image
exploring the long
distances some
commuters are
travelling to their
place of work

Lyndon Hayes
Party 1

M Acrylic, collage

B To create a series
of images depicting
urban themes that
represent modern
youth culture

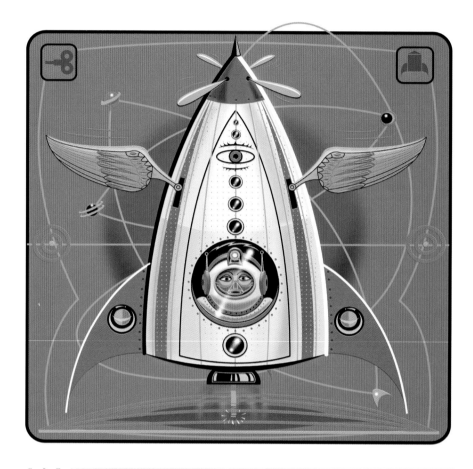

Tony Healey

Howlin' Wolf

M Watercolour

B One of a set of twelve
Blues / Jazz portraits
for an exhibition to
coincide with the
Brecon International
Jazz Festival 2003

BB King

M Watercolour

B One of a set of twelve
Blues / Jazz portraits
for an exhibition to
coincide with the
Brecon International
Jazz Festival 2003

Anthony Hibbert
Foreign Parts
M Mixed media
B To create a moody
but fun image
while continuing
development of
my personal style

David Hitch

A Million Manias

M Digital

B A self initiated
project to illustrate
as many strange
phobias as possible

Darren Hopes

Songbird

M Mixed media

B Interpretation
of music. One in a
series, source of
inspiration - 'Songbird'
by Bernard Moss
on the Park Label

Darren Hopes

Like Eels		Airhead	
M	Mixed media	M	Mixed media
B	Inspired by a gut wrenching passage from the book Humanity, a modern history of the 20th Century by Jonathan Glover	B	One in a series of music-inspired illustrations. This one forms the cover of a CD mixed by myself of all the pieces of music used as a source of inspiration for this collection of illustrations

David Humphries

Hello! Goodbye!

M Digital

B Self initiated piece
about celebrity
culture and the media
perception of the
other passengers
in Diana's car

Rod Hunt

American Diner

M Digital

B Promotional mailer

Stuart Jones
Road to Hell

M Acrylic on
watercolour

B To create a graphic
novel without words;
this is a panel
illustration from
the novel influenced
by heaven and hell

Rita Kearton

My Green Daughter

M   Handcoloured dry
    point print. Limited
    edition 20.

B   Illustrate the children's
    poem 'My Green
    Daughter': In the cold
    river under the water
    by the dark stones lies
    my green daughter.
    Poet: James Birch

Sarah Lawrence

Buddha

M   Watercolour
    & gold leaf

B   Speculative work

Richard Levesley
The Little Imp

M Mixed media

B To design an image
that works on a large
scale incorporating
text & image, using
the theme of losing
objects

Beware of
Strong Currents

M Mixed media

B To produce a series
of images exploring
the theme currents

Henning Löhlein

Puzzle

M   Acrylic

B   The tedious art of
doing jigsaw puzzles

Greg as a Giraffe

M   Acrylic

B   Greg is a sheep with
a big imagination
and he imagines to
be different animals

Greg as a Bee

M   Acrylic

B   Greg is a sheep with
a big imagination
and he imagines to
be different animals

Loon
Travel

M Mixed media

B Development
of travel journal.
Images from
Marrakesh,
Kathmandu and
Coney Island,
New York

Mark Marshall
Little Lost Lion 1
M Acrylic
B Speculative image from my own children's book

Little Lost Lion 2
M Acrylic
B Speculative image from my own children's book

Robbie Loxston
Jelly Beany
M Digital
B Working up new style with a highly commercial subject matter.

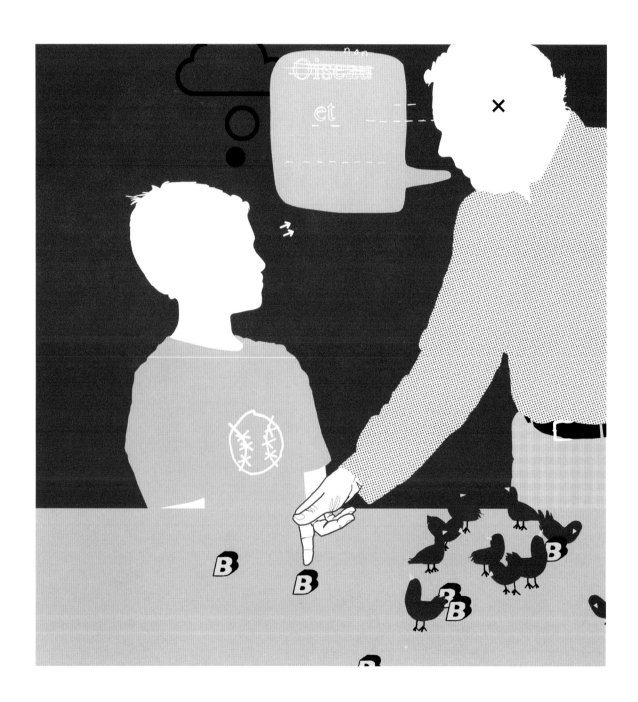

Shane McGowan
Circus
M Digital
B Self promotion
piece for my agent

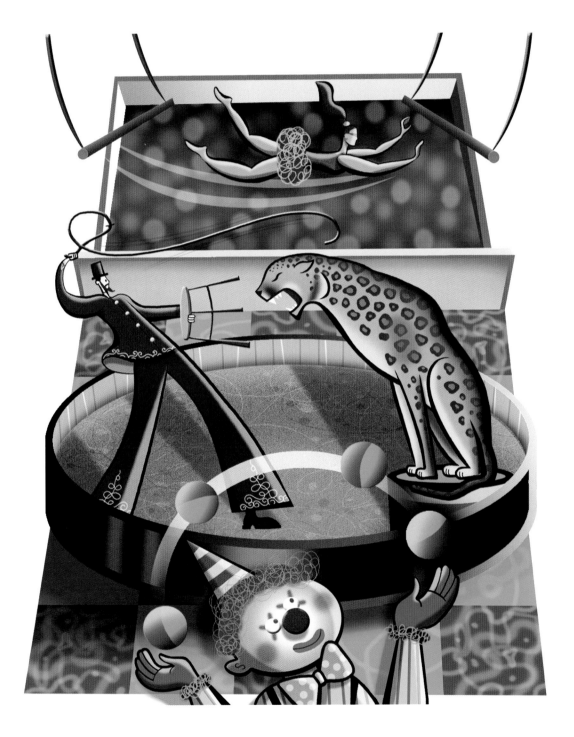

C Holly Venable
F Three In A Box

Sunday 2nd September

In the middle of the night the Baker woke up with a start.
He coughed and choked on thick billowing smoke as he scrambled out of bed.
He quickly threw on some clothes and ran to the window. Flames licked hungrily
at the stairs. The Baker clambered out on to the roof, along the gutter and across
to the next door neighbour's garret.

The flames that had fed on the flour and kindling in the bakery crept through
the house, consuming wood panelling, furniture, clothes and curtains.
The fire shattered the horsehair plaster walls, the weather-boarding
and the window panes. Soon the whole of the Baker's house was ablaze.

At first people on the street tried to help. They looked for the fire-fighting equipment
stored in the nearby church, but found that most of it was broken or missing.
The water supply was really low because of the drought and no one was prepared
to walk all the way down to the river. Soon the neighbours abandoned the few fire squirts
and buckets they had found and concentrated on saving their own things, storing them in
the church.

A footman woke the Mayor.
He got up and reluctantly went to see what all the
fuss was about. Pudding Lane was too narrow for his
carriage. He was really fed up. The Mayor decided the
fire wasn't big enough to warrant his help.

Julia Midgley
Huyton Playground

M Acrylic ink

B Record through
drawing life in
Huyton, Merseyside
for Liverpool Biennial
and Knowsley
Borough 2002

Julia Midgley
Floodlit Tennis
M Acrylic ink
B Poster illustration
for local tennis
club seeking funds
for floodlights

Helen Mills
Eating Out in London

M Gouache

B To produce an
image to represent
the culture of eating
out in London by
bus, tube and river.
Produced for the
SAA Illustration
Awards 2004

F SAA / London
Transport

Liz Minichiello

St Petersburg Spring

M Ink, conté & pencil

B Personal response
to the end of winter
in St Petersburg
coinciding with the
cleaning campaign
in preparation for
the May 2003
City Anniversary
Celebration

Spring Cleaning
in St Petersburg

M Ink & gouache paint

B Re-laying
Palace Square,
the Hermitage,
St Petersberg

David Martin Morrison
South Bank

M   Digital

B   Self promotional piece

Sally Newton
Work vs Play

M Digital

B Reponse to article
on extending your
working life to retire
at 70, reducing the
'Golden Years'
in which you finally
escape and enjoy life

Michael O'Shaughnessy
Whatever Happened
to Peace and Quiet?

M Mixed media

B Unpublished
commission

Su Owen
No Charge
For Delivery

M Collage, acrylic
  & fabric

B Self promotional work

Paquebot
Cheese

M Digital

B Fashion shoot
  for mice

Paquebot

Is Red Wine Good
For Your Heart?

M Digital

B There are claims and
counter claims about
red wine's benefit
to your heart

Bad Tempered
Luggage

M Digital

B Some badly
packed suitcases
pose problems for
luggage handlers

Gossip

M Digital

B Illustrate how a
gossip spreads

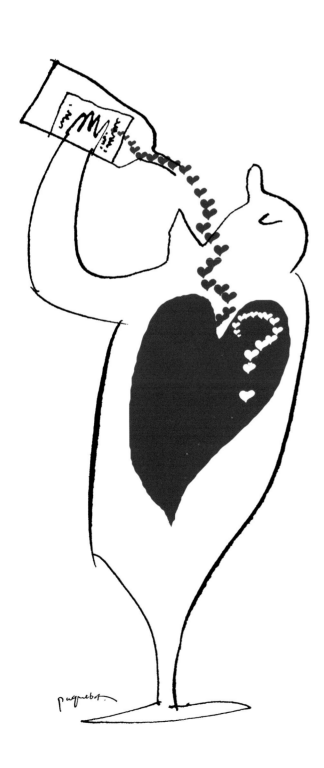

Ducks in the City
M Digital
B Illustrate ducks
walking in
the city street

9 Lives
(or Cat's Dilemma)
M Digital
B A cat contemplates
it's next move in
front of a moving car,
but having too many
(nine) options hinders
it's decision, hence life

Liberty & The Mole
M Digital
B Civil liberty may be at
risk as moles monitor
society's every move

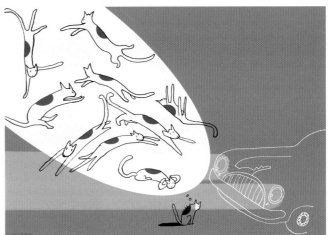

Jacqui Paull
Citroen
M Mixed media
B Personal work

Emma Peascod
Christopher Walken

M Pen, ink &
digital media

B To create a portrait /
caricature of
Christopher Walken

Sally Pinhey
June Wayside
Flowers

M Watercolour

B Collection of common
wild flowers. Dorset
botanical artists
illustrated a selection
of Dorset wild flowers
for a special exhibition
to celebrate the
centenary of botanist
JC Mansel-Pleydel

Ian Pollock
Mary Annoints Jesus

M Pen and ink (line and wash) & collage

B Pollock's New Testament - one of fifty-five illustrations for the New Testament, for exhibition at the EICH Gallery, Hull

Paul Ratcliffe
Postman

M Acrylic

Unpublished
Silver award winner

B Personal brief
illustrating a letter
about re-directed
mail which was
being sent to the old
address rather than
the address it had
been re-directed to

Matthew Richardson

Stratford Boys

M Mixed media

B To illustrate the cover
of 'Stratford Boys'
by Jan Mark: A
humorous, fictional
account of the
teenage Shakespeare
producing his very first
(undiscovered) play

C David McDougall

F Hodder Children's
Books

Harriet Russell
Levi's Worn Jeans

M Screenprint and pencil

B Speculative
piece for Levi's, in
response to their 'rub
yourself' campaign
for worn jeans

Lorna Siviter
Non-Run to the Sun

M Digital

B Part of series
depicting the
ups and downs
of summer travel

Matthew Skilton
Do Androids Dream
of Electric Sheep?

M Digital

B Bookjacket for the
Philip K Dick science-
fiction novel

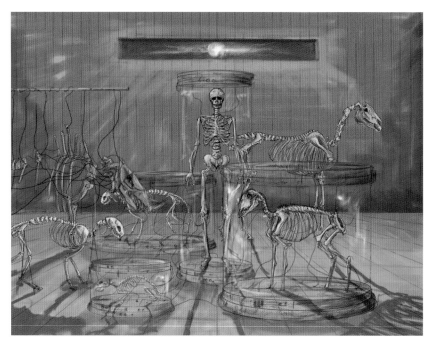

Jason Stavrou

Nick Cave

M Pen and ink (digital)

B To illustrate Nick Cave

Self Portrait

M Pen and ink

B To come up with
a self portrait

Orange

Grey

Purple

C Marc Lawrence

F Eyecandy

Anna Steinberg

Hot Horses

M Ink

B Personal work

Deborah Stephens

Living Memory

M Digital

B Opening sequences
to a narrative.
A couple's relationship
is compared from
1958 Soho clubland
to their retirement
in contemporary
suburbia

Josephine Sumner
The Hound of Odin

M Scraperboard

B To illustrate the
Wiltshire Legend
of the 'Black Dog'
and its Nordic origins

**Daniela Jaglenka
Terrazzini**

September Fairy

M Watercolour and
pressed flowers

B Personal project,
series of 12 fairies
accompanied
by short poems

August Fairy

M Watercolour and
pressed flowers

B Personal project,
series of 12 fairies
accompanied
by short poems

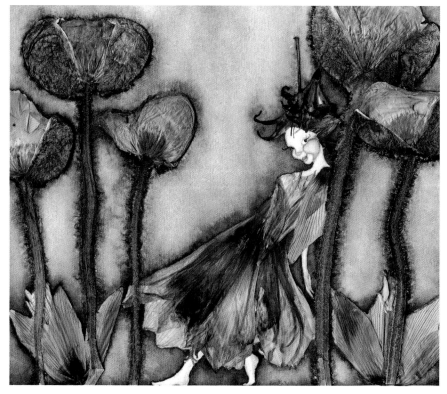

Samuel Thomas
Oops!

M Acrylic

B Produce a piece of
work to demonstrate
in full colour the style
and to maintain the
interest of the viewer

Michelle Thompson
Eating Out

M Collage

B To produce an
artwork, suitable
for use as a poster
for Transport for
London designed to
inform all Londoners
of the variety of places
to eat out in London

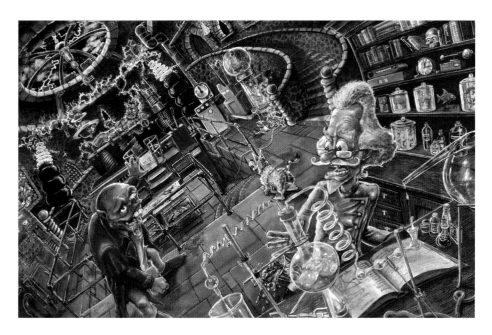

Gerry Turley
Lord of the Flies
M   Watercolour & ink
B   Self-motivated brief
    to illustrate cover
    of 'Lord of the Flies'
    by William Golding

Dominic Turnbull
T-Halving Joint
in Mahogany
M   Acrylic
B   Experimental

Tony Watson
Global Warning
M   Acrylics & digital
B   What could happen
     if the world's ice-caps
     continue to shrink

Jane Webster
Venice Café
M   Pencil
B   Location drawing
     of Venice café culture

Steven Whitaker
Cowboy
M Oils
B Originally this painting was for the door of the men's room in a cowboy-themed pub in the north of England

Scale

M Oils

B To illustrate
the word 'scale

Lu Willis
Fun and Games!

M Gouache

B A drawing to
illustrate how a local
infant school now
represents its local
community a century
after it first opened

Lorna Woodland
Bull

M Collage

B Produce a series
of horoscopes
aimed at a young
male audience,
using sport/leisure
to represent star
signs. Self promotion

AOI **membership** benefits

The Association of Illustrators provides a voice for professional illustrators and by force of numbers and expertise is able to enforce the rights of freelance illustrators at every stage of their careers. Membership of the AOI is open to all illustrators, illustration students, agents, colleges and illustration clients.

All categories of membership receive the following benefits:
- Bimonthly journal
- Discounted rate for Images – competition entries, hanging fees and annual pages
- Contact details on office database for enquiries from clients
- Discounts from material suppliers
- Discounts on AOI events and publications.

In addition we provide the following services for particular types of membership:

Full membership
This category is for professional illustrators who have had work commissioned and accept the AOI code of conduct:
- Legal advice on contracts
- Information on pricing and professional practice
- Free portfolio surgery
- Business advice – an hour's free consultation with a chartered accountant on accounts, book-keeping, National Insurance, VAT and tax
- Full members are entitled to use the affix 'Mem AOI'
- Discounts on AOI events, publications and online ImageFile

Associate membership
The benefits are the same as those for full membership but this one-year category is for newcomers and illustrators on their first year out of college who have not yet published work. In exceptional circumstances this membership can be extended by an extra year:

Student membership
This service is for students on full-time illustration or related courses:
- Advice on entering the profession
- Free portfolio consultation
- Bimonthly journal
- Large discounts on AOI events, publications and competition entry
- Discounts on art materials

Corporate membership
This service is for agents and clients from the illustration industry who adhere to the AOI code of conduct.
- Bimonthly journal
- Free copy of the Images annual
- All corporate members' staff and illustrators will receive discounts on events, Images and AOI publications

College membership
College membership entitles the college to the following benefits:
- Bimonthly journal
- Large discounts on AOI events and publications
- Link to college web page from AOI site
- Copy of Images illustration annual
- The right to use the AOI member logo on publicity

Additional options (at extra cost) include:
- Portfolio consultations
- Illustrator lecture
- Discount on bulk orders of additional copies of the bimonthly Journal, Rights & Survive
- Degree show presence on AOI website

For an application form and cost details please contact:
Association of Illustrators
81 Leonard Street
London EC2A 4QS

T +44 (0)20 7613 4328
F +44 (0)20 7613 4417

E info@theaoi.com
W www.theAOI.com

AOI publications
Survive: The illustrators Guide to a Professional Career
Published by the AOI and revised 2001, Survive is the only comprehensive and in-depth guide to illustration as a professional career. Established illustrators, agents, clients and a range of other professionals have contributed to this fourth edition. Each area of the profession including portfolio presentation, self-promotion and copyright issues are looked at in detail. The wealth of information in Survive makes it absolutely indispensable to the newcomer and also has much to offer the more experienced illustrator.

Rights: The Illustrators Guide to Professional Practice
Rights is an all inclusive guide to aspects of the law specifically related to illustration. It includes information about copyright, contracts, book publishing agreements, agency agreements, how to go about seeking legal advice, how to calculate fees and guidance on how to write a licence. Rights is the result of a number of years research. It has been approved by solicitors and contains the most detailed and accurate model terms and conditions available for use by illustrators or clients.

Troubleshooting Guide
A handbook written by solicitors Ruth Gladwin and Robert Lands (Finers Stephens Innocent) covering essential legal issues surrounding subjects such as animation, collage, websites, and advice about taking cases to the small claims court.

Client Directories
We publish three directories Publishing, Advertising and Editorial each containing over 180 commissioners of illustration with full contact details – providing an invaluable source of information for all practitioners.

www.theaoi.com

www.aoiimages.com

Evolving year on year theAOI.com is the definitive resource for UK illustrators. The site is comprised of four main sections:

News and information
Regularly updated news page and full information about the Association. Sub-sections include: Membership, Personnel, Rights, Ethics Code, Publications, and Downloads. There is also an extensive links page with lists of both UK/overseas agencies, publishers, advertising agencies and international groups.

Articles
Archive of texts drawn predominantly from the AOI's Journal publication. Individual issues of the Journal can be browsed or use the search facility to locate specific texts. Articles are also categorised under various industry headings i.e. agents, professional practice, legal, education etc.

Discussion
The AOI Discussion Board is a moderated board open for all to read and post. After registering, users can reply to existing messages or start new topics. Images and links can also be included with messages. The Board has eight forums including Professional Practice, AOI Feedback, Tools of the Trade, General, Archive, Polls (where users can vote on issues of the day) and a separate forum for AOI members only.

Events
An online calendar featuring daily and monthly views of all events of interest to the illustration community. Visitors are invited to submit content for inclusion.

Launched in 2003 AOImages.com was specifically developed to promote illustration to the creative industries. Currently featuring over 3000 images and growing fast, the site is made up of three sections:

ImageFile
The ImageFile is, in part, a permanent and growing collection of published works categorised by industry usage. Images are tagged for speedy retrieval utilising a number of different search criteria. ImageFile also includes the Portfolio section which enables illustrators to manage their own online portfolio of up to 20 images. Illustrators have options to upload images, delete, edit caption info, and more, from the convenience of their own computer.

Images book
Recent Images annuals, in their entirety, online and searchable.

Directory
The Directory provides direct links to the work of illustrators whether on their own site or within their agent's or other corporate site. Now linking to the portfolios of over 700 illustrators.

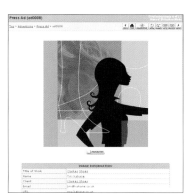

The AOI Journal

The essential illustration magazine

The AOI Journal, re-launched in Summer 2000, covers a wide range of issues related to the illustration industry including:

- Current industry affairs
- Illustration events
- Reviews
- Interviews
- Letters

Regular contributors include practitioners, educators and industry professionals. The Journal provides a forum for on-going debate, and a valuable insight into contemporary illustration.

Published six times a year. Free to members. To subscribe to the AOI Journal as a non-member, please send your cheque for £30, made payable to the Association of Illustrators, to:

Journal Subscription
AOI
81 Leonard Street
London EC2A 4QS

For payment by Visa, Mastercard or Switch
T +44 (0)20 7613 4328

index of illustrators

About the illustrators

A Agent
T Telephone
F Fax
M Mobile
E Email
W Website

To call from outside
the UK add the prefix '44'
and omit the first '0' from
the number provided

Scott Chambers 207
109 Battery Road
Thamesmead
London SE28 OJW
T 020 8855 5447
M 07790 420 367
E info@scott
   chambers.co.uk
W www.scott
   chambers.co.uk
A Synergy
103C Clarendon Road
London W11 4JG
T 020 7727 9800
W www.synergyart.co.uk

John Charlesworth 208
72 Frost Street
Ettingshall, Wolverhampton
Staffordshire WV2 2LL
T 01902 498 308
M 07960 676 943
E jc@john
   charlesworth.com
W www.john
   charlesworth.com

Nishant Choksi 209
5 Todd House
The Grange, East Finchley
London N2 8NL
M 07855 362 694
E nish@nishantchoksi.com
W www.nishantchoksi.com

Greg Clarke 31
A The Artworks
70 Rosaline Road
London SW6 7QT
T 020 7610 1801
F 020 7610 1811
E lucy@theartworksinc.com
W www.theartworksinc.com

Russell Cobb 17,32,152,
210,211
The Studio, St Bridgets
Radcliffe Road, Hitchin
Hertfordshire SG5 1QH
T 01462 441 614
F 01462 441 614
M 07961 414 613
E russell@russellcobb.com
W www.russellcobb.com

Miles Cole 76
74 Engel Park, Mill Hill
London NW7 2HP
T 020 8349 3364
F 020 8349 3364
M 07970 746 781
E milesc@dircon.co.uk
W www.milesc.dircon.co.uk

Matthew Cook 77
A The Artworks
70 Rosaline Road
London SW6 7QT
T 020 7610 1801
F 020 7610 1811
E lucy@theartworksinc.com
W www.theartworksinc.com

Nicky Cooney 211
30 Stanley Road
Oxford OX4 1QZ
T 01865 242 166
E nicky@nickycooney.com
W www.nickycooney.com

Paul Cox 78
A Arena
108 Leonard Street
London EC2A 4RH
T 020 7613 4040
F 020 7613 1441
E info@arenaworks.com
W www.arenaworks.com

Jonathan Croft 212
T 01444 461 996
M 07944 343 365
E jonathan.croft
   @btinternet.com
W www.3illustrators.co.uk

Mel Croft 212
T 01444 461 996
M 07939 037 239
E mel.croft@btinternet.com
W www.3illustrators.co.uk
A Eye Candy Illustration
Agency, 15 Frobisher Court
Sydenham Rise
London SE23 3XH
T 020 8291 0729
F 020 8291 2964
E marc.lawrence
   @eyecandy.co.uk
W www.eyecandy.co.uk

Brian Cronin 79
59 West 12th Street
Apt # 8H,
10011 New York, USA
T 001 212 727 9539
E brian@briancronin.com
W www.briancronin.com

Jonathan Cusick 33–35,
80,81
10 Wynyates
Sageside, Tamworth
Staffordshire B79 7UP
T 01827 50003
F 01827 50003
E theboss
   @jonathancusick.com
W www.jonathancusick.com

Clémence de Limburg 176
avenue de Lothier 3
B-1150 Bruxelles, Belgium
M 00 32 472 352 868
E clembzzz@hotmail.com

Cyrus Deboo 82,83
57 Ormonde Court
Upper Richmond Road
London SW15 6TP
T 020 8788 8167
F 020 8788 8167
M 07050 039 477
E cyrus.deboo@virgin.net
W www.cyrusdeboo.com

Nick Dewar 83
E nick.dewar@verizon.net
A Eastwing
99 Chase Side
Enfield EN2 6NL
T 020 8367 6760
F 020 8367 6730
E andrea@eastwing.co.uk
W www.eastwing.co.uk

Philip Disley 84
7 Parkgate Close, Aigburth
Liverpool L17 6EH
T 0151 494 1604
F 0151 494 1604
M 07779 783 414
E phil.disley@virgin.net
W www.kastaris.com

Jovan Djordjevic 85
9 Fairlop Road
Leytonstone
London E11 1BL
T 020 8520 4011
F 020 8520 9866
M 07788 778 296
E jovan@
   jovan.demon.co.uk
W www.jovandjordjevic.com

Ian Dodds 213
18 Ramsey Close
Rubery, Rednal
Birmingham B45 0HQ
T 0121 453 2802
M 07905 243 739
E contact@iandodds.co.uk
W www.iandodds.co.uk
A Meiklejohn Illustration
5 Risborough Street
London SE1 0HF
T 020 7593 0500
F 020 7593 0501
E paul@meiklejohn.co.uk
W www.meiklejohn.co.uk

Jane Donald 177
30 Potash Road, Billericay
Essex CM11 1DL
T 01277 650 086
M 07779 221 062
E janedonald21
   @hotmail.com

Barry Downard 17,36
A Début Art
30 Tottenham Street
London W1T 4RJ
T 020 7636 1064
F 020 7580 7017
E debutart@coningsby
   gallery.demon.co.uk
W www.debutart.com

Sarah Dyer 86,136
Flat 9
Balham Park Mansions
Balham Park Road
London SW12 8DY
T 020 8673 1895
M 07811 420 821
E sahrdyer@hotmail.com
A Eye Candy Illustration
Agency, 15 Frobisher Court
Sydenham Rise
London SE23 3XH
T 020 8291 0729
F 020 8291 2964
E marc.lawrence
   @eyecandy.co.uk
W www.eyecandy.co.uk

Kate Edmunds 214
6 Glentworth Road
Clifton Wood
Bristol BS8 4TB
T 0117 927 7747
M 07879 460 003
E egg.nogg@virgin.net
W www.eggnogg.co.uk

Stephen Elford 214
Upper Maisonette
131 Preston Drove
Brighton
East Sussex BN1 6LE
T 01273 503 552
F 08701 389 614
M 07808 293 756
E steve@elfpix.co.uk
W www.elfpix.co.uk

Max Ellis 18,86,87
60 Clonmel Road
Teddington
Middlesex TW11 0SR
T 020 8977 8924
F 020 8241 6289
M 07976 242 378
E max@junkyard.co.uk
W www.killerpixel.com
A Central Illustration Agency
36 Wellington Street
London WC2E 7BD
T 020 7240 8925
F 020 7836 1177
E info@central
   illustration.com
W www.central
   illustration.com

Sara Fanelli 37,136
Flat 11 Howitt Close
Howitt Road
London NW3 4LX
T 020 7483 2544
F 020 7483 2544
E sara@sarafanelli.com

Ben Farnell 177
34 Sholing Road
Southampton
Hampshire SO19 2ED
T 023 8032 6879
M 07752 393 188
E uberdada@aol.com
W www.uberdada.com

David Fathers 38
32 Hollyfield Avenue
Friern Barnet
London N11 3BY
T 020 8368 8516
M 07905 075 057
E david@joemoon.co.uk
W www.joemoon.co.uk

Johanna Fernihough 215
A Début Art
30 Tottenham Street
London W1T 4RJ
T 020 7636 1064
F 020 7580 7017
E debutart@coningsby
   gallery.demon.co.uk
W www.debutart.com

Kirstie Fitzgerald 215
6 Thornby Avenue, Solihull
West Midlands B91 2BJ
T 0121 705 3835
M 07855 572 544
E fitzgeraldkirstie
   @hotmail.com

Jason Ford 88
T 020 7923 4433
M 07779 032 156
E j.ford@macunlimited.net
A Heart, Top Floor
100 De Beauvoir Road
London N1 4EN
T 020 7254 5558
F 020 7923 4791
E info@heartagency.com
W www.heartagency.com

Andrew Foster 88
M 07966 283 237
E foz@dircon.co.uk

James Fryer 89,90,91
Flat 5, Fernbank House
Portsmouth Road
Thames Ditton
Surrey KT7 0SY
T 020 8873 0923
F 020 8873 0923
M 07812 672 819
E james_fryer72
   @hotmail.com

Sarah Gibb 39,153
A The Artworks
70 Rosaline Road
London SW6 7QT
T 020 7610 1801
F 020 7610 1811
E lucy@theartworksinc.com
W www.theartworksinc.com

Sarah Gill 137
35 B Leigh Road
London N5 1AH
T 020 7226 9097
M 07985 456 341
E inkcap@zoom.co.uk

Rachel Goslin 216
6 Cadogan Road
Royal Arsenal
London SE18 6SN
T 020 8316 5785
F 020 8316 5785
M 07740 168 969
E rachelgoslin123
   @hotmail.com
A Eye Candy Illustration
Agency, 15 Frobisher Court
Sydenham Rise
London SE23 3XH
T 020 8291 0729
F 020 8291 2964
E marc.lawrence
   @eyecandy.co.uk
W www.eyecandy.co.uk

Vincent Gould 216
27 Bradbury Road
Olton, Solihull
West Midlands B92 8AE
T 0121 706 9287
M 07816 452 676
E vincentgould
@hotmail.com

Carolyn Gowdy 92
2c Maynard Close
Off Cambria Street
London SW6 2EN
T 020 7731 5380
E cgowdy@attglobal.net

Adam Graff 92,217
10 St Columbas House
16 Prospect Hill
London E17 3EZ
T 020 8521 7182
F 020 8521 7182
M 07747 196 811
E a.graff@ntlworld.com

Geoff Grandfield 93
30 Allen Road
London N16 8SA
T 020 7241 1523
F 020 7241 1523
M 07831 534 192

Willi Gray 154
9 York Street, Norwich
Norfolk NR2 2AN
T 01603 499 928
M 07960 896 037
E gris.gris@ntlworld.com

Philip Grisewood 178
23 Ethelwulf Road
Worthing
West Sussex BN14 7NF
T 07746 796 477
M 07905 872 969
E philipgrisewood
@hotmail.com

Peter Grundy 218,219
Grundy & Northedge
Power Road Studios
114 Power Road
London W4 5PY
T 020 8995 2452
E peter@grundy
northedge.com
W www.grundy
northedge.com

Kayo Harada 179
140 Westbourne Terrace
Paddington
London W2 6QD
M 07796 384 009
E kayo_harada
@hotmail.com
A Monster Illustration
T 020 8769 3667
W www.monsters.co.uk

Nick Hardcastle
40,155–157
April Cottage, The Rosery
Mulbarton, Norwich
Norfolk NR14 8AL
T 01508 570 153
F 01508 570 153
M 07973 144 696
E nickhardcastle
@supanet.com

Jo Hassall 41
A Private View Art Agency
17a Swan Hill
Shrewsbury SY1 1NL
T 01743 350 355
F 01743 233 923
E create@pvuk.com
W www.pvuk.com

Lynn Hatzius 157
30 Belfast Road
London N16 6UH
T 020 7502 2010
M 07949 385 446
E info@yseye.de
W www.yseye.de
A Monster Illustration
W www.monsters.co.uk

Kevin Hauff 220
1 Kingwood Avenue
Heaton, Bolton
Lancashire BL1 5JA
T 01204 842 859
F 01204 842 859
M 07866 339 893
E info@kevinhauff.com
W www.kevinhauff.com

Ben Hawkes 179
Top Flat, 51 Saltoun Road
Brixton, London SW2 1EW
T 020 7326 0390
M 07960 117 415
E washout1@hotmail.com

Lyndon Hayes 220
15 Kings Grove, Peckham
London SE15 2LY
T 020 7732 8274
M 07890 104 779
E theelyndonhayes
@lyndonscircus.co.uk
W www.lyndonscircus.co.uk

Tony Healey 221
TH Illustration Ltd
T 020 7071 2334
F 020 7071 1064
M 07721 460 411
E tony.healey@
arcmarketing.com
W www.th-illustration.co.uk
A Art Collection
25 The Crescent
Manchester M5 4PF
T 0870 240 5001
F 0870 240 5002
E info@artcollection.co.uk
W www.artcollection.co.uk

Eva-Kajsa Hedström 180
37 King Charles Road
Surbiton, Surrey KT5 8NY
T 020 8399 0721
M 07753 217 448
E evakajsasbigtrain_78
@hotmail.com

Matt Herring 94,158
Unit E1A
Upper Bounds Green Ind
Estate, The Ringway
London N11 2UD
T 020 8361 4913
F 020 8361 4913
M 07970 283 576
E matt@mattherring.com
W www.mattherring.com

Anthony Hibbert 222
Oxford, England
M 07905 941 046
E anthonyhib@hotmail.com
W www.anthony-
hibbert.co.uk

David Hitch 223
A Arena
108 Leonard Street
London EC2A 4RH
T 020 7613 4040
F 020 7613 1441
E info@arenaworks.com
W www.arenaworks.com

Darren Hopes 19,223,224
A Début Art
30 Tottenham Street
London W1T 4RJ
T 020 7636 1064
F 020 7580 7017
E debutart@coningsby
gallery.demon.co.uk
W www.debutart.com

Mark Hudson 44
7 Maria Terrace
London E1 4NE
T 020 7253 2807
M 07970 712 345
E m.hudson.esq@virgin.net

Peter Horridge 42,43,95
Maribonne, Bunbury Lane
Bunbury, Tarporley
Cheshire CW6 9QS
T 01829 261 801
F 01829 261 801
M 07775 583 760
E peter@horridge.com
W www.horridge.com
A Central Illustration Agency
36 Wellington Street
London WC2E 7BD
T 020 7240 8925
F 020 7836 1177
E info@central
illustration.com
W www.central
illustration.com

Sarah Howe 181
35 Sovereign Court
Southfields Road
Loughborough
Leicestershire LE11 2TL
M 07813 110 934
E sarahchowe
@hotmail.com
W www.21illustrators.co.uk
W www.contact-
me.net/dollymixtures

Suzanna Hubbard 138
2 Lime Tree Cottages
Vicarage Road, Shrewsbury
Shropshire SY3 9HA
T 01743 244 578
F 01743 244 578
M 07939 025 003
E zanna.hubbard@virgin.net
A David Higham Associates
5-8 Lower John Street
Golden Square
London W1F 9HA
T 020 7434 5900
F 020 7437 1072
E lucyfirth@
davidhigham.co.uk
W www.davidhigham.co.uk

Frazer Hudson 96,97
354 Manchester Road
Sheffield
South Yorkshire S10 5DQ
T 0114 268 2861
M 07973 616 054
E frazer@dircon.co.uk
W www.frazer.dircon.co.uk

Rian Hughes 159
Device, 2 Blake Mews
Kew, Surrey TW9 3QA
T 020 8896 0626
M 07979 602 272
E rianhughes@aol.com
W www.devicefonts.co.uk

David Humphries
98,99,225
6 Merton Road
Walthamstow
London E17 9DE
T 020 8503 6012
F 020 8503 6012
M 07973 831 724
E david@monsters.co.uk
A Monster
W www.monsters.co.uk

Rod Hunt 100,225
63 Ashburnham Place
Greenwich
London SE10 8UG
T 020 8469 0472
F 020 8469 0472
M 07931 588 750
E rod@rodhunt.com
W www.rodhunt.com

Adrian Johnson 101
67 Farringdon Road
London EC1
T 020 7430 0722
F 020 7430 0722
M 07958 670 750
E info@adrian
johnson.org.uk
W www.adrian
johnson.org.uk
A Central Illustration Agency
36 Wellington Street
London WC2E 7BD
T 020 7240 8925
F 020 7836 1177
E info@central
illustration.com
W www.central
illustration.com

Peter Jones 160
72 Forthill Road
Broughty Ferry
Dundee DD5 3DN
T 01382 738 444
E p.jones@dundee.ac.uk

Stuart Jones 226
c/o 75 Beaufort Hill
Beaufort, Ebbw Vale
Gwent NP23 5QW
T 01495 305 448
M 07931 478 704
E smjonesillustrator
@hotmail.com

Satoshi Kambayashi
102–104
Flat 2, 40 Tisbury Road
Hove, East Sussex BN3 3BA
T 01273 771 539
F 01273 771 539
M 0773 917 9107
E satoshi.k@virgin.net
W www.satillus.com

Rita Kearton 227
4 Winnold Cottages
Fincham Road
Wereham, King's Lynn
Norfolk PE33 9AB
T 01366 347 664
E ritakearton@
ritakearton.com
W www.ritakearton.com

Roy Knipe 105
A Thorogood Illustration
5 Dryden Street
London WC2E 9NW
T 020 7829 8468
F 020 7497 1300
E draw@thorogood.net
W www.thorogood.net

Olivier Kugler 62
W www.olivierkugler.com
A The Artworks
70 Rosaline Road
London SW6 7QT
T 020 7610 1801
F 020 7610 1811
E lucy@theartworksinc.com
W www.theartworksinc.com

Cameron Law 105
61 Mountearl Gardens
Streatham
London SW16 2NN
T 020 8769 3667
M 07950 433 922
E cam.law@virgin.net
A Monster Illustration
W www.monsters.co.uk

Sarah Lawrence 227
3 Parkfield Cottages
Parkfield Cross, Ashburton
Devon TQ13 7ND
T 01364 652 931
M 0845 456 1705
M 07729 629 844
E sarahlawrence
@freeuk.com

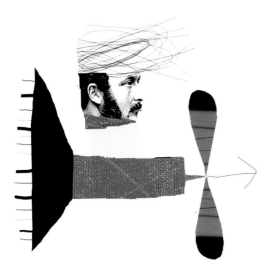

Matt Lee 19,106
33 Sherbrooke Road
Fulham, London SW6 7QJ
T 020 7610 1585
M 07759 984 669
E mail@matt-lee.com
W www.matt-lee.com
A Eye Candy Illustration
Agency, 15 Frobisher Court
Sydenham Rise
London SE23 3XH
T 020 8291 0729
F 020 8291 2964
E marc.lawrence
    @eyecandy.co.uk
W www.eyecandy.co.uk

Sean Lee 107
T 01316 574 369

Toby Leigh 108
59 Elmar Road
London N15 5DH
M 07976 939 853
E tobatron@hotmail.com
A Folio10 Gate Street
Lincoln's Inn Fields
London WC2A 3HP
T 020 7242 9562
F 020 7242 1816
E all@folioart.co.uk
W www.folioart.co.uk

Richard Levesley 228
94 Coltsfoot Green
Luton, Bedfordshire
LU4 0XT
T 01582 668 258
M 07729 532 324
E richard@
    levesley.fsnet.co.uk
W www.jprwhite
    .co.uk/richard

Henning Löhlein 229
Centre Space
6 Leonard Lane
Bristol BS1 1EA
T 0117 929 9077
F 0117 929 9077
M 07711 285 202
E Henning@Lohlein.com
W www.Lohlein.com

Loon 230
44 Marlborough Drive
Clayhall, Essex IG5 0JW
T 020 8520 9617
M 07714 757 855
E loon.moon@ntlworld.com

Leonie Lord 160
43 London Road
Cheltenham
Gloucestershire GL52 6HE
T 01242 517 153
E leonielord.illustration
    @virgin.net
A The Inkshed
99 Chase Side
Enfield EN2 6NL
T 020 8367 4545
F 020 8367 6730
E abby@inkshed.co.uk
W www.inkshed.co.uk

Frank Love 109
the dairy studios
5-7 Marischal Road
London SE13 5LE
T 020 8297 2212
F 020 8297 1680
M 07930 492 471
E thedairy@btclick.com
W www.franklove.co.uk
A Eastwing
99 Chase Side
Enfield EN2 6NL
T 020 8367 6760
F 020 8367 6730
E andrea@eastwing.co.uk
W www.eastwing.co.uk

Robbie Loxston 231
43 Ham Hill
Stoke-sub-Hamdon
Somerset TA14 6RW
T 01935 824 015
M 07971 075 041
E robillus@tantraweb.co.uk
A New Division
5 Risborough Street
London SE1 0HF
T 020 7593 0505
F 020 7593 0501
E paula@newdivision.com
W www.newdivision.com

Richard Lyon 161
10 Greenland Close
North Anston
Sheffield S25 4AW
T 01909 562 544
M 07979 935 559
E richard_lyon70
    @hotmail.com
W www.richardlyon.com

Michelle MacRae 182
3rd Floor
100 Annfield Road
Dundee DD1 5JH
T 01382 566 957
M 07960 231 608
E miladyprinneth
    @supanet.com

Warren Madill 110
5 Risborough Street
London SE1 0HF
T 020 7593 0500
F 020 7593 0501

Peter Malone 161
A The Artworks
70 Rosaline Road
London SW6 7QT
T 020 7610 1801
F 020 7610 1811
E lucy@theartworksinc.com
W www.theartworksinc.com

Daniel Marcolin 110,111
The Garden Flat
45 Courthope Road
London NW3 2LE
T 020 7267 4406
F 020 7267 4406
M 07974 919 364
E daniel_marcolin
    @yahoo.co.uk

Mark Marshall 231
Clockwork Studios
38A Southwell Road
Camberwell
London SE5 9PG
T 020 7924 0921
F 020 7924 0921
M 07985 648 655
E mark@mmarshall
    7.fsnet.co.uk
A Eunice McMullen
Low Ibbotsholme Cottage
Off Bridge Lane
Troutbeck Bridge
Windemere Cumbria
LA23 1HU
T 01539 448 551
E eunicemcmullen
    @totalise.co.uk

Mei Matsuoka 183
57 Lime Avenue
Buckingham
Buckinghamshire MK18 7JJ
T 01280 813 357
M 07939 230 684
E meiski@hotmail.com
A PFD Alison Kain
Drury House
34 - 43 Russell Street
London WC2B 5HA
T 020 7344 1056
F 020 7836 9539
E akain@pfd.co.uk
W www.pfd.co.uk

Ian Pollock 48,118, 249
171 Bond Street
Macclesfield
Cheshire SK11 6RE
T   01625 426 205
F   01625 426 205
M 07770 927 940
E   ianpllck@aol.com
W www.ianpollock.
plus.com
A   The Inkshed
99 Chase Side
Enfield EN2 6NL
T   020 8367 4545
F   020 8367 6730
E   abby@inkshed.co.uk
W www.inkshed.co.uk

Ashley Potter 49
the dairy studios
5-7 Marischal Road
London SE13 5LE
T   020 8297 2212
F   020 8297 1680
M 07930 492 471
E   thedairy@btclick.com
W www.thedairy
studios.co.uk

Paul Powis 49
Four Seasons
Battenhall Avenue
Worcester
Worcestershire
WR5 2HW
T   01905 357 563
F   01905 357 563
E   haywardpowis
@hotmail.com
W www.powis
hayward.com

Lisa Raftery 185
9 Burleigh Road
Loughborough
Leicestershire LE11 3BA
M 07984 254 257
E   lisa@lisaraftery.com
W www.lisaraftery.com

Paul Ratcliffe 250
1 Yew Tree Cottages
Sheepscombe, Stroud
Gloucestershire GL6 7RB
T   01452 813 854
M 07764 493 014
E   paul@seemybits.com
W www.paulillustration
anddesign.co.uk

Matthew Richardson
119, 251
Garden Cottage
Penpont, Brecon
Powys LD3 8EU
T   01874 636 269
F   01874 636 269
E   matthewxr@aol.com
A   Eastwing
99 Chase Side
Enfield EN2 6NL
T   020 8367 6760
F   020 8367 6730
E   andrea@eastwing.co.uk
W www.eastwing.co.uk

Erika Richmond 186
40 Granville Road
Tunbridge Wells
Kent TN1 2NX
T   01892 529 386
M 07810 452 819
E   erika-uk@talk21.com
W www.dandad.org
/bloodbank

Chris Robson 120
55 Kellaway Avenue
Westbury Park
Bristol BS6 7XS
T   0117 942 5918
M 07971 379 354
E   chris@chrisrobson.com
W www.chrisrobson.com

Paul Rogers 164
W www.paulrogers
studio.com
A   The Artworks
70 Rosaline Road
London SW6 7QT
T   020 7610 1801
F   020 7610 1811
E   lucy@theartworksinc.com
W www.theartworksinc.com

Rachel Ross 165
A   The Inkshed
99 Chase Side
Enfield EN2 6NL
T   020 8367 4545
F   020 8367 6730
E   abby@inkshed.co.uk
W www.inkshed.co.uk

Harriet Russell
50,121,252
Flat 4, 175 Sussex Gardens
London W2 2RH
Happiness at Work
1 Green Bank, Wapping
London, E1W 2PA
T   020 7262 7318 (h)
T   020 7480 5638 (s)
M 07977 151 277
E   harriet77@clara.co.uk

Bill Sanderson 165
Fernleigh
Huntingdon Road, Houghton
Cambridgeshire PE28 2AU
T   01480 461 506
F   01480 461 506
E   art@billsandersonart.com
W www.billsanderson
art.com

Rosie Scott 186
130 Westbourne Street
Hove, East Sussex
BN3 5FB
T   01273 324 613
M 07951 191 051
E   rosiebethscott@aol.com

Susan Scott 144
Flat 2/1
12 Yorkhill Street
Glasgow G3 8SB
T   0141 339 5170
F   0141 339 5170
M 07799 480 776
E   susan.scott4
@btinternet.com
W www.scottish
illustrators.com
W www.chooseillustration.
com/susan_scott

Colin Shearing 51
108 Hammersmith Grove
London W6 7HB
M 07956 198 672
E   shearing@dircon.co.uk

Michael Sheehy 52,121
115 Crystal Palace Road
East Dulwich
London SE22 9ES
T   020 8693 4315
F   020 8693 4315
M 07814 587 136
E   michael.sheehy
@btinternet.com

Lucie Sheridan 187
Poplar Cottage
School Road
Windlesham
Surrey GU20 6PA
M 07887 723 749
E   lucieloo@lucie
sheridan.co.uk
W www.lucie
sheridan.co.uk
A   Eastwing
99 Chase Side
Enfield EN2 6NL
T   020 8367 6760
F   020 8367 6730
E   andrea@eastwing.co.uk
W www.eastwing.co.uk

Lorna Siviter 252
1 Nightingale Acre
Hatch Beauchamp
Taunton Somerset TA3 6TF
T   01823 481 469
M 07901 961 474
E   lorna.siviter@virgin.net
A   Eastwing
99 Chase Side
Enfield EN2 6NL
T   020 8367 6760
F   020 8367 6730
E   andrea@eastwing.co.uk
W www.eastwing.co.uk

Lasse Skarbovik 122,150
A   The Organisation
69 Caledonian Road
Kings Cross
London N1 9BT
T   020 7833 8268
F   020 7833 8269
E   organise@easynet.co.uk
W www.organisart.co.uk

Matthew Skilton 252
134 The Avenue
West Wickham
Kent BR4 0EA
T   020 8777 4216
M 07941 627 598
E   mattskilton@
mattskilton.co.uk
W www.mattskilton.co.uk

Mark Slack 188
16 Troon Way, Hinckley
Leicestershire LE10 2GX
T   01455 637 408
M 07967 610 884
E   slackym@yahoo.co.uk
W www.markslack.co.uk

Czeslaw Slania 52
Sweden Post Stamps
SE–164 88 Kista, Sweden
T   00 46 (0) 8 781 5490
E   hans.nyman
@pf.posten.se

Paul Slater 53,122,123
22 Partridge Close
Chesham
Buckinghamshire HP5 3LH
T   01494 786 780
F   01494 786 780
E   paulslater@
btinternet.com
W www.cuttergallery.com

**Benjamin
Bogart Small** 189
68 Rosemont Road
Liverpool L17 6DA
T   0151 724 3868
M 07817 603 072
E   benbogart@hotmail.com

Andy Smith 200
A   Private View Art Agency
17a Swan Hill
Shrewsbury SY1 1NL
T   01743 350 355
F   01743 233 923
E   create@pvuk.com
W www.pvuk.com

Phil Smith 190
18 Stockwell Road
Knaresborough
North Yorkshire HG5 0JZ
T   01423 861 153
M 07970 998 374
E   phil-smith@fsmail.net
W www.philsmith
portfolio.com

Ray Smith 20
M 07906 252 320
E   r.smith@c2i.net
W www.raysmith.bz

Nobby Sprouts 53
the dairy studios
5-7 Marischal Road
London SE13 5LE
T   020 8297 2212
F   020 8297 1680
M 07930 492 471
E   thedairy@btclick.com
W www.thedairy
studios.co.uk

Julia Staite 190
15 Stonard Road
Palmers Green
London N13 4DJ
T   020 8882 1068
M 07740 355 262
E   jce_staite@hotmail.com
W www.juliastaite.com

Jason Stavrou 253
18 Northbrook Road
Bowes Park
London N22 8YQ
T   020 8881 7621
M 07989 364 648
E   jason.stavrou@virgin.net
W www.jasonstavrou.com
A   Eye Candy Illustration
Agency, 15 Frobisher Court
Sydenham Rise
London SE23 3XH
T   020 8291 0729
M 07811 363 718
E   marc.lawrence
@eyecandy.co.uk
W www.eyecandy.co.uk

Anna Steinberg 254
6 Langler Road
London NW10 5TL
T   020 8964 1069
F   020 8964 1069
M 07890 882 252
E   a.steinberg
@btopenworld.com
W www.annasteinberg.co.uk

Deborah Stephens 254
7 George Court
Kings Place, Buckhurst Hill
Essex IG9 5HR
T   020 8504 6081
M 07798 828 123
E   deborah.stephens
@talk21.com

Christina Stone 190
Rose Cottage, The Street
Swanton Abbott
Norfolk NR10 5DU
T   01692 538 559
E   markstone@
tinyworld.co.uk
W www.christinastone-
illustrator.co.uk

Josephine Sumner
124, 255
16 Nursteed Road
Devizes, Wiltshire
SN10 3AH
T   01380 728 873
E   josephine@
josephinesumner.com
W www.josephine
sumner.com

Sharon Tancredi 170,191
8 Loraine Road, Holloway
London N7 6EZ
T   020 7700 0278
M 07802 481 459
E   s.tancredi@
btinternet.com
W www.sharontancredi.com

David Tazzyman 125
A Private View Art Agency
17a Swan Hill
Shrewsbury SY1 1NL
T 01743 350 355
F 01743 233 923
E create@pvuk.com
W www.pvuk.com

Daniela Jaglenka Terrazzini 256
M 07816 880 803
E daniela@jaglenka.
plus.com

Samuel Thomas 257
344 St John's Lane
Bedminster
Bristol BS3 5BA
T 0117 377 5817
M 07867 562 775
E mynameissam
@hotmail.com

Michelle Thompson 257
59 High Street
Saffron Walden
Essex CB10 1AA
T 01799 523 229
F 01799 523 229
M 07956 180 211
E michellethompson.
studio@btinternet.com
W www.contact-me.net/
MichelleThompson

Naomi Tipping 192–194
14 Jarvis Avenue
Bakersfield
Nottingham NG3 7BH
T 0115 911 5996
M 07968 194 095
E naomitipping
@hotmail.com
W www.naomitipping.com

Jago Titcomb 195
5 Clapper Farm Flats
Egloshayle, Wadebridge
Cornwall PL27 6HZ
T 01208 812 441
E jago@earthling.net
W www.jagoillustration.com

Tobatron (Toby Leigh) 126
59 Elmar Road
London N15 5DH
M 07976 939 853
E tobatron@hotmail.com
A Folio, 10 Gate Street
Lincoln's Inn Fields
London WC2A 3HP
T 020 7242 9562
F 020 7242 1816
E all@folioart.co.uk
W www.folioart.co.uk

Nancy Tolford 126
20 Park Road, Walthamstow
London E17 7QF
T 020 8520 9204
F 020 8520 9204
M 07905 748 281
E nancy@nancytolford.com
W www.nancytolford.com

Corrin Tulk 196
14 Wilton Road
Muswell Hill
London N10 1LS
M 07813 516 703
E info@illustrationart.org
W www.illustrationart.org

Gerry Turley 258
84 Putney Park Lane, Putney
London SW15 5HN
T 020 8516 7901
F 020 8516 7901
M 07815 997 247
E gryturley@aol.com

Dominic Turnbull 258
135 Vernon Road
Poynton, Stockport
Cheshire SK12 1YS
T 01625 879 932
M 07958 739 337
E domturnbull
@yahoo.co.uk

Helen Turner 196,197
22 Spring Close
Ebchester, Consett
County Durham DH8 0QL
T 01207 563 069
M 07779 583 063
E turnerpictures@aol.com

Bob Venables 20,126
109 Tuam Road
London SE18 2QY
T 020 8316 0223
F 020 8316 0223
M 07752 437 487
E robert.venables1
@btopenworld.com
W http://homepage.mac.
com/robertvenables
/photoalbum5.html
A Thorogood Illustration
5 Dryden Street
London WC2E 9NW
T 020 8859 7507
F 020 8333 7677
E draw@thorogood.net
W www.thorogood.net

Stefano Vitale 127
Santa Croce 1012
I-30135 Venice, Italy
T 00 39 041 719 273
F 00 39 041 719 273
E stefanovitale@aol.com

Darrell Warner 54
The Old Farmhouse
Preston, Cirencester
Gloucestershire GL7 5PR
T 01285 653 405
F 01285 651 152
M 07881 877 854

Peter Warner 55,166,167
Peter Warner's Studio
Hillside Road, Tatsfield
Kent TN16 2NH
T 01959 577 270
F 01959 577 271
M 07958 531 538
E thestudio@
peterwarner.com
W www.peterwarner.com

Stephen Waterhouse 145
2A Norwood Grove
Birkenshaw, Bradford
West Yorkshire BD11 2NP
T 01274 875 892
F 01274 875 892
M 07971 347 856
E stephen@stephen
waterhouse.com
W www.stephen
waterhouse.com

Tony Watson 259
124 Cambridge Street
Wolverton, Milton Keynes
MK12 5AQ
T 01908 316 273
F 01908 316 273
E tony@tonywatson.net
W www.tonywatson.net

Paul Wearing 56,57
PW Art Limited
Unit B4, Metropolitan Wharf
Wapping Wall
London E1W 3SS
T 020 7481 4653
F 020 7481 4654
E paulwearing@
illustrator.demon.co.uk

Jane Webster 127,259
A Début Art
30 Tottenham Street
London W1T 4RJ
T 020 7636 1064
F 020 7580 7017
E debutart@coningsby
gallery.demon.co.uk
W www.debutart.com

Louise Weir 21,58,59
Studio 32
10 Martello Street
London Fields
London E8 3PE
T 020 7923 9639
F 020 7923 9639
M 07966 284 090
E louise@louiseweir.com
W www.louiseweir.com

Chris West 128
First Floor
12 Dorset Street
London W1U 6QS
T 020 7486 6253
F 020 7027 2137
E west@duewest.co.uk

Ian Whadcock 24,129,168
M 07967 119 058
E art@ianwhadcock.com
A Eastwing
99 Chase Side
Enfield EN2 6NL
T 020 8367 6760
F 020 8367 6730
E andrea@eastwing.co.uk
W www.eastwing.co.uk

Steven Whitaker 260,261
9 Chelsham Road
London SW4 6NR
T 020 7622 5419
F 020 7622 5419
E stevenwhitaker
@btinternet.com
W www.steven-
whitaker.com

Donat Willenz 198
The Old Malthouse
Unit 3A, Level 2, Clarence
Street, Bath BA1 5NS
M 07816 552 673
E donatwillenz
@hotmail.com

Bee Willey 60,144
A Illustration Ltd
2 Brooks Court
Cringle Street
London SW8 5BX
T 020 7720 5202
F 020 7720 5920
E harry@illustration
web.com
W www.illustration
web.com

Jonathan Williams 130,131
United Kingdom
T 01651 891 876
F 01651 891 876
M 07867 526 477
E jon@blazingfruit.com
W www.portfolios.
com/JonathanWilliams

Lu Willis 261
42 Courtlands,
Maidenhead
Berkshire SL6 2PU
T 01628 623 327
F 01928 623 327
M 07799 756 289
E luwillis7824
@hotmail.com

Anne Wilson 146,147
38 Chester Street
Reading Berkshire
RG30 1LP
T 0118 958 9446
M 07050 129 038
A Illustration Ltd
2 Brooks Court
Cringle Street
London SW8 5BX
T 020 7720 5202
F 020 7720 5920
E team@illustration
web.com
W www.illustration
web.com

Lee Woodgate 131
Flat 2, Old Well House
The Grove, London N6 6LD
T 020 8340 0315
F 020 8340 0315
M 07979 657 392
E lee@leewoodgate.com
W www.leewoodgate.com
A Eye Candy Illustration
Agency, 15 Frobisher Court
Sydenham Rise
London SE23 3XH
T 020 8291 0729
F 020 8291 2964
E marc.lawrence@
eyecandy.co.uk
W www.eyecandy.co.uk

Lorna Woodland 262
18 Moulin Avenue
Southsea
Hampshire PO5 2RF
M 07980 577 745
E pinkcustardxxx
@hotmail.com

Christopher Wormell 22,148
A The Artworks
70 Rosaline Road
London SW6 7QT
T 020 7610 1801
F 020 7610 1811
E lucy@theartworksinc.com
W www.theartworksinc.com

Philip Wrigglesworth 132
7 Standroyd Drive
Colne, Lancashire
BB8 7BG
T 01282 864 884
M 07939 794 267
E wooillustrations
@hotmail.com
W www.woo
illustrations.co.uk